CAMBRIDGE ESSAYS

ON

EDUCATION

T0371199

CAMBRIDGE ESSAYS
ON
EDUCATION

EDITED BY

A. C. BENSON, C.V.O., LL.D.

MASTER OF MAGDALENE COLLEGE

WITH AN INTRODUCTION BY THE RIGHT HON.
VISCOUNT BRYCE, O.M.

CAMBRIDGE
AT THE UNIVERSITY PRESS
1917

CAMBRIDGE
UNIVERSITY PRESS

University Printing House, Cambridge CB2 8BS, United Kingdom

Published in the United States of America by Cambridge University Press, New York

Cambridge University Press is part of the University of Cambridge.

It furthers the University's mission by disseminating knowledge in the pursuit of
education, learning and research at the highest international levels of excellence.

www.cambridge.org
Information on this title: www.cambridge.org/9781107698406

First published 1917
First paperback edition 2014

A catalogue record for this publication is available from the British Library

ISBN 978-1-107-69840-6 Paperback

PREFACE

THE scheme of publishing a volume of essays dealing with underlying aims and principles of education was originated by the University Press Syndicate. It seemed to promise something both of use and interest, and the further arrangements were entrusted to a small Committee, with myself as secretary and acting editor.

Our idea has been this: at a time of much educational enterprise and unrest, we believed that it would be advisable to collect the opinions of a few experienced teachers and administrators upon certain questions of the theory and motive of education which lie a little beneath the surface.

To deal with current and practical problems does not seem the *first* need at present. Just now, work is both common as well as fashionable; most people are doing their best; and, if anything, the danger is that organisation should outrun foresight and intelligence. Moreover a weakening of the old compulsion of the classics has resulted, not in perfect freedom, but in a tendency on the part of some scientific enthusiasts simply to substitute compulsory science for compulsory literature, when the real question rather is whether obligatory subjects should not be diminished as far as possible, and more sympathetic attention given to faculty and aptitude.

We have attempted to avoid mere current controversial topics, and to encourage our contributors to define as far as possible the aim and outlook of education, as the word is now interpreted.

We have not furthered any educational conspiracy, nor attempted any fusion of view. Our plan has been first to select some of the most pressing of modern problems, next to find well-equipped experts and students to deal with each, and then to give the various writers as free a hand as possible, desiring them to speak with the utmost frankness and personal candour. We have not directed the plan or treatment or scope of any essay; and my own editorial supervision has consisted merely in making detailed suggestions on smaller points, in exhorting contributors to be punctual and diligent, and generally revising what the New Testament calls jots and tittles. We have been very fortunate in meeting with but few refusals, and our contributors readily responded to the wish which we expressed, that they should write from the personal rather than from the judicial point of view, and follow their own chosen method of treatment.

We take the opportunity of expressing our obligations to all who have helped us, and to Viscount Bryce for bestowing, as few are so justly entitled to do, an educational benediction upon our scheme and volume.

A. C. BENSON

Magdalene College, Cambridge
August 18, 1917

CONTENTS

INTRODUCTION   ix
By the Right Hon. VISCOUNT BRYCE, O.M.

I.   THE AIM OF EDUCATIONAL REFORM .   I
By JOHN LEWIS PATON, M.A., High Master of
Manchester Grammar School; formerly Fellow of
St John's College, Cambridge, Assistant Master at
Rugby School, Head Master of University College
School

II.   THE TRAINING OF THE REASON . .   12
By the Very Rev. WILLIAM RALPH INGE, D.D.,
Dean of St Paul's, Honorary Fellow of Jesus College,
Cambridge, and of Hertford College, Oxford;
formerly Lady Margaret Professor of Divinity,
Fellow of King's College, Cambridge, Assistant
Master at Eton College, Fellow and Tutor of
Hertford College, Oxford

III.   THE TRAINING OF THE IMAGINATION   34
By ARTHUR CHRISTOPHER BENSON, C.V.O.,
LL.D., Master of Magdalene College, Cambridge;
formerly Assistant Master at Eton College

IV.   RELIGION AT SCHOOL   53
By WILLIAM WYAMAR VAUGHAN, M.A., Master
of Wellington College; formerly Assistant Master
at Clifton College, and Head Master of Giggleswick
School

V.   CITIZENSHIP   75
By ALBERT MANSBRIDGE, M.A., Joint-Secretary
of the Cambridge University Tutorial Classes
Committee; Founder and formerly Secretary of
the Workers' Educational Association

VI.   THE PLACE OF LITERATURE IN EDU-
CATION 102
By NOWELL SMITH, M.A., Head Master of
Sherborne School; formerly Fellow of Magdalen
College, Oxford, Fellow and Tutor of New College,
Oxford, Assistant Master at Winchester College

VII.   THE PLACE OF SCIENCE IN EDUCATION 121
By WILLIAM BATESON, F.R.S., Director of the
John Innes Horticultural Institution, Honorary
Fellow of St John's College, Cambridge; formerly
Professor of Biology in the University of Cambridge

VIII.   ATHLETICS 148
By FREDERIC BLAGDEN MALIM, M.A., Master
of Haileybury College; formerly Assistant Master
at Marlborough College, Head Master of Sedbergh
School

IX.   THE USE OF LEISURE 168
By JOHN HADEN BADLEY, M.A., Head Master of
Bedales School

X.   PREPARATION FOR PRACTICAL LIFE . 188
By Sir JOHN DAVID McCLURE, LL.D., D.Mus.,
Head Master of Mill Hill School

XI.   TEACHING AS A PROFESSION . . . 215
By FRANK ROSCOE, Secretary of the Teachers
Registration Council

INTRODUCTION

IN times of anxiety and discontent, when discontent has engendered the belief that great and widespread economic and social changes are needed, there is a risk that men or States may act hastily, rushing to new schemes which seem promising chiefly because they are new, catching at expedients that have a superficial air of practicality, and forgetting the general theory upon which practical plans should be based. At such moments there is special need for the restatement and enforcement by argument of sound principles. To such principles so far as they relate to education it is the aim of these essays to recall the public mind. They cover so many branches of educational theory and deal with them so fully and clearly, being the work of skilled and vigorous thinkers, that it would be idle for me to enter in a short introduction upon those topics which they have discussed with special knowledge far greater than I possess. All I shall attempt is to present a few scattered observations on the general problems of education as they stand to-day.

The largest of those problems, viz., how to provide elementary instruction for the whole population, is far less urgent now than it was fifty years ago. The Act of 1870, followed by the Act which made school-attendance compulsory, has done its work. What is wanted now is Quality rather than Quantity. Quantity is doubtless needed in one respect. Children ought to stay longer at school and ought to have more encouragement to continue education after they leave the elementary school. But it is chiefly an improvement in the teaching that is wanted, and that of course means the securing of higher competence in the teacher by raising the remuneration and the status of the teaching profession[1].

The next problem is how to find the finest minds among the children of the country and bring them by adequate training to the highest efficiency. The sifting out of these best minds is a matter of educational organisation and machinery; and the process will become the easier when the elementary teachers, who ought to bear a part in selecting those who are most fitted to be sent on to secondary schools, have themselves become better qualified for the task of discrimination. The question how to train these best minds when sifted out would lead me into the tangled controversy as to the respective educational values of various subjects of instruction, a topic which I must not deal with here. What I do wish to dwell upon is the supreme importance to the progress of a nation of the best talent it possesses. In every country there is a certain percentage of the population who are fitted by their superior intelligence, industry, and force of character to be the leaders in every

[1] This has been clearly seen and admirably stated by the present President of the Board of Education.

branch of action and thought. It is a small percentage, but it may be increased by discovering ability in places where the conditions do not favour its development, and setting it where it will have a better chance of growth, just as a seedling tree brought out of the dry shade may shoot up when planted where sun and rain can reach it freely. I am not thinking of those exceptionally great and powerful minds, of whom there may not be more than four or five in a generation, who make brilliant discoveries or change the currents of thought, but rather of persons of a capacity high, if not quite first rate, which enables them, granted fair chances, to rise quickly into positions where they can effectively serve the community. These men, whatever occupation they follow, be it that of abstract thinking, or literary production, or scientific research, or the conduct of affairs, whether commercial or political or administrative, are the dynamic strength of the country when they enter manhood, and its realised wealth when they are in their fullest vigour thirty years later. We need more of them, and more of them may be found by taking pains.

The volume of thought continuously applied to the work of life, whether it be applied in the library or study or laboratory, or in the workshop or factory or counting-house or council chamber, has not been keeping pace with the growth of our population, our wealth, our responsibilities. It is not to-day sufficient for the increasing vastness and complexity of the problems that confront a great nation. We in Great

Britain have been too apt to rely upon our energy and courage and practical resourcefulness in emergencies, and thus have tended to neglect those efforts to accumulate knowledge, and consider how it can be most usefully applied, which should precede and accompany action. This deficiency is happily one that can be removed, while a want of qualities which are the gift of nature is less curable. The "efficiency" which is on every one's mouth cannot be extemporised by rushing hastily into action, however energetic. It is the fruit of patient and exact determination of and reflection upon the facts to be dealt with.

The view that it was the finest minds that ought to be most cared for, and that to them of right belonged not merely leadership, but even control also, was carried by the ancients, and especially by Plato and Aristotle, almost to excess. Their ideal, and indeed that of most Greek thinkers, was the maintenance among the masses of the military valour and discipline which the State needed for its protection, and the cultivation among the chosen few of the highest intellectual and moral excellence. In the Middle Ages, when power as well as rank belonged to two classes, nobles and clergy, the ideal of education took a religious colour, and that training was most valued which made men loyal to the Church and to sound doctrine, with the prospect of bliss in the world to come. In our times, educational ideals have become not merely more earthly but more material. Modern doctrines of equality have discredited the ancient view that the chief aim of instruction is to prepare the few

Wise and Good for the government of the State. It is not merely upon this world but also upon the material things of this world, power and the acquisition of territory, industrial production, commerce, finance, wealth and prosperity in all its forms, that the modern eye is fixed. There has been a drifting away from that respect for learning which was strong in the Middle Ages and lasted down into the eighteenth century. In some countries, as in our own, that which instruction and training may accomplish has been rated far below the standard of the ancients. Yet in our own time we have seen two striking examples to show that their estimate was hardly too high. Think of the power which the constant holding up, during long centuries, of certain ideals and standards of conduct, exerted upon the Japanese people, instilling sentiments of loyalty to the sovereign and inspiring a certain conception of chivalric duty which Europe did not reach even when monarchy and chivalry stood highest. Think of that boundless devotion to the State as an omnipotent and all-absorbing power, superseding morality and suppressing the individual, which within the short span of two generations has taken possession of Germany. In the latter case at least the incessant preaching and teaching of a theory which lowers the citizen's independence and individuality while it saps his moral sense seems to us a misdirection of educational effort. But in it education has at least displayed its power.

Can a fair statement of the educational ideals which we might here and now set before ourselves be found in saying that there are three chief aims to be sought as respects those we have called the best minds?

One aim is to fit men to be at least explorers, even if not discoverers, in the fields of science and learning.

A second is to fit them to be leaders in the field of action, leaders not only by their initiative and their diligence, but also by the power and the habit of turning a full stream of thought and knowledge upon whatever work they have to do.

A third is to give them the taste for, and the habit of enjoying, intellectual pleasures.

Many moralists, ancient and modern, have given pleasure a bad name, because they saw that the most alluring and powerfully seductive pleasures, pleasures which appeal to all men alike, were indulged to excess, and became a source of evil. But men will have pleasure and ought to have pleasure. The best way of drawing them off from the more dangerous pleasures is to teach them to enjoy the better kinds. Moreover the quieter pleasures of the intellect mean Rest, and a greater fitness for resuming work.

The pity is that so many sources capable of affording delight are ignored or imperfectly appreciated. May not this be partly the fault of the lines which our education has followed? Perhaps some kinds of study would have fared better if their defenders had dwelt more upon the pleasure they afford and less upon their supposed utility. The champions of Greek and Latin have dilated on the value of grammar as a mental discipline, and argued that the best way to acquire a good English style is to know the ancient

languages, a proposition discredited by many examples
to the contrary. It is really this insistence on grammatical minutiae that has proved repellent to young
people, and suggested the dictum that "it doesn't
much matter what you teach a boy so long as he
hates it." Better had it been, abandoning the notion
that every one should learn Greek, to dwell upon the
boundless pleasure which minds of imagination and
literary taste derive from carrying in memory the gems
of ancient wisdom which are more easily remembered
because they are not in our own language, and the
finest passages of ancient poetry. There are plenty
of things—indeed there are far more things—in
modern literature as noble and as beautiful as the
best of the ancients can give us. But they are not
the same things. The ancient poets have the freshness and the fragrance of the springtime of the world[1].

Or take another sort of instance. Take the
pleasures which nature spreads before us with a
generous hand, hills and fields and woods and rocks,
flowers and the songs of birds, the ever-shifting
aspects of clouds and of landscapes under light and
shadow. How few persons in most countries—for

---

[1] Take for instance this little fragment of Alcman:

Οὔ μ' ἔτι, παρθενικαὶ μελιγάρυες ἱμερόφωνοι,
Γυῖα φέρειν δύναται· βάλε δὴ βάλε κηρύλος εἴην,
Ὅς τ' ἐπὶ κύματος ἄνθος ἅμ' ἀλκυόνεσσι ποτῆται
Νηλεγὲς ἦτορ ἔχων, ἁλιπόρφυρος εἴαρος ὄρνις.

What can be more exquisite than the epithets in the first line, or more
fresh and delicate and tender in imaginative quality than the three last?
A modern poet of equal genius would treat the topic with equal force and
grace, but the charm, the untranslatable charm of antique simplicity,
would be absent.

there is in this respect a difference between different peoples—notice these things. Everybody sees them, few observe them or derive pleasure from them. Is not this largely because attention has not been properly called to them? They have not been taught to look at natural objects closely and see the variety there is in them. Persons in whom no taste for pictures has ever been formed by their having been taken to see good pictures and told what constitutes merit, are, when led into a picture gallery, usually interested in the subjects. They like to see a sportsman shooting wild fowl, or a battle scene, or even a prize fight, or a mother tending a sick child, because these incidents appeal to them. But they seldom see in a picture anything but the subject; they do not appreciate imaginative quality or composition, or colour, or light and shade or indeed anything except exact imitation of the actual. So in nature the average man is struck by something so exceptional as a lofty rock, like Ailsa Craig or the Needles off the Isle of Wight, or an eclipse of the moon, or perhaps a blood-red sunset; but he does not notice and consequently draws no pleasure from landscapes in general, whether noble or quietly beautiful. The capacity for taking pleasure in all these things may not be absent. There is reason to think that most children possess it, because when they are shown how to observe they usually respond, quickly perceiving, for instance, the differences between one flower and another, quickly, even when quite young, learning the distinctive characters and names of each, enjoying the process of recognising each when they walk along the lanes, as indeed every intelligent child enjoys the exercise of its observing powers. The disproportionate growth of our urban population, a thing regrettable in other respects also, has no doubt made it more difficult to give young people a familiar knowledge of nature, but the facilities for going into the country and the happy lengthening of summer holidays render it easier than formerly to provide opportunities for Nature Study, which, properly conducted, is a recreation and not a lesson. There is no source of enjoyment which lasts so keen all through life or which fits one better for other enjoyments, such as those of art and of travel. Of the value of the habit of alert observation for other purposes I say nothing, wishing here to insist only upon what it may do for delight.

It is often alleged that in England boys and girls show less mental curiosity, less desire for knowledge than those of most European countries, or even than those of the three smaller countries north and west of England in which the Celtic element is stronger than it is in South Britain. A parallel charge has, ever since the days of Matthew Arnold, been brought against the English upper and middle classes. He declared that they care less for the "things of the mind" and show less respect to eminence in science, literature and art, than is the case elsewhere, as for instance in France, Germany, or Italy (to which one may add the United States); and he thus explained the scanty interest taken by these classes in educational progress.

Should this latter charge be well founded, the fact it notes would tend to perpetuate the former evil, for the indifference of parents reacts upon the school and upon the pupils. The love of knowledge is so natural, and awakens so early in the normal child, that even if it be somewhat less keen among English than among French or Scottish children, we may well believe our deficiencies to be largely due to faulty and unstimulative methods of teaching, and may trust that they will diminish when these methods have been improved.

If it be true that the English public generally show a want of interest in and faint appreciation of the value of education, the stern discipline of war will do something to remove this indifference. The comparative poverty and reduction of luxurious habits which this war will bring in its train, along with a sense of the need that has arisen for turning to the fullest account all the intellectual resources of the country so that it may maintain its place in the world,—these things may be expected to work a change for the better, and lead parents to set more store upon the mental and less upon the athletic achievements of their sons.

Be this as it may, no one to-day denies that much remains to be done to spread a sense of the value of science for those branches of industry to which (as especially to agriculture) it has been imperfectly applied, to strengthen and develop the teaching of scientific theory as the foundation of technical and practical scientific work, and above all to equip with the largest measure of knowledge and by the most stimulating training those on whom nature has bestowed the most vigorous and flexible minds. To-day we see that the heads of great businesses, industrial and financial, are looking out for men of university distinction to be placed in responsible posts—a thing which did not happen fifty years ago—because the conditions of modern business have grown too intricate to be handled by any but the best trained brains. The same need is at least equally true of many branches of that administrative work which is now being thrust, in growing volume, upon the State and its officials.

If we feel this as respects the internal economic life of our country, is it not true also of the international life of the world? In the stress and competition of our times, the future belongs to the nations that recognise the worth of Knowledge and Thought, and best understand how to apply the accumulated experience of the past. In the long run it is knowledge and wisdom that rule the world, not knowledge only, but knowledge applied with that width of view and sympathetic comprehension of men, and of other nations, which are the essence of statesmanship.

I

THE AIM OF EDUCATIONAL REFORM

By J. L. PATON

High Master of Manchester Grammar School

The last century, with all its brilliant achievement in scientific discovery and increase of production, was spiritually a failure. The sadness of that spiritual failure crushed the heart of Clough, turned Carlyle from a thinker into a scold, and Matthew Arnold from a poet into a writer of prose.

The secret of failure was that the great forces which move mankind were out of touch with each other, and furnished no mutual support. Art had no vital relation with industry; work was dissociated from joy; political economy was at issue with humanity; science was at daggers drawn with religion; action did not correspond to thought, being to seeming; and finally the individual was conceived as having claims and interests at variance with the claims and interests of the society of which he formed a part, in fact as standing out against it, in an opposition so sharply marked that one of the greatest thinkers could write a book with the title "Man *versus* the State." As a result, nation was divided against nation, labour against capital, town against country, sex against sex, the hearts of the children were set against the fathers, the Church fought against the State, and, worst of all, Church fought against Church.

The discords of the great society were reflected inevitably in the sphere of education. The elementary schools of the nation were divided into two conflicting groups, and both were separated by an estranging gulf from the grammar schools and high schools, as the grammar schools in turn were shut off from the public schools on the one hand, and from the schools of art, music, and of technology on the other. There was no cohesion, no concerted effort, no mutual support, no great plan of advance, no homologating idea.

This fact in itself is sufficient to account for the ineffectiveness, the despondencies, the insincerities, and ceaseless unrest of Western civilisation in the nineteenth century. The tree of human life cannot flower and bear fruit for the healing of the nations, when its great life-forces spend themselves in making war on each other.

If the experience of the century which lies before us is to be different, it must be made so by means of education. Education is the science which deals with the world as it is capable of becoming. Other sciences deal with things as they are, and formulate the laws which they find to prevail in things as they are. The eyes of education are fixed always upon the future, and philosophy of whatever kind, directly it adumbrates a Utopia, thinks on educational lines.

The aim of education must therefore be as wide as it is high, it must be co-extensive with life. The advance must be along the whole front, not on a small sector only. William Morris, when he tried his hand at painting, used to say, that what bothered him always was the frame: he could not conceive of art as something "framed off" and isolated from life. Just as William Morris wanted to turn all life into art, so with education. It cannot be "framed off" and detached from the larger aspects of political and social well-being; it takes all life for its province. It is not an end in itself, any more than the individuals with whom it deals; it acts upon the individual, but through the individual it acts upon the mass, and its aim is nothing less than the right ordering of human society.

To cope with a task which can be stated in these terms, education must be free. A new age postulates a new education. The traditions which have dominated hitherto must one by one be challenged to render account of themselves, that which is good in them must be conserved and assimilated, that which is effete must be scrapped and rejected. Neither can the administrative machinery, as it exists, be taken for granted; unless it shows those powers of adaptation and growth which show it to be alive and not dead, it too must be scrapped and rejected; new wine is fatal to old skins. Education must regain once more what she possessed at the time of the Renascence —the power of direction; she must be mistress of her fate.

Further, if education is to be a force which makes for co-operation in place of conflict, she must not be divided against herself. She must leave behind for ever the separations and snobberies, the misunderstandings, the wordy battles beloved of pedants and politicians. The smoke and dust of controversy obscures her vision, and she needs all her energies to tackle the great task which confronts her. In this regard nothing is so full of promise for the future as the new sense of unity which is beginning both to animate and actuate the whole teaching profession, from the University to the Kindergarten, and has already eventuated in the formation of a Teachers Registration Council, on which all sorts and conditions of education are represented.

The materialists have not been slow to see their chance, to challenge the old tradition of literary education, and to urge the claims of science. But the aim which they place before us is frankly stated—it is the acquisition of wealth; they are "on manna bent and mortal ends," and their conception of the future is a world in which one nation competes against another for the acquisition of markets and commodities. In effect, therefore, materialism challenges the classics, but it accepts the self-seeking ideals of the past generations, and accepts also, as an integral part of the future, the scramble of conflicting interests, labour against capital, nation against nation, man against man. Now the first characteristic of the genuine scientific mind is the power of learning by experience. Real science never makes the same mistake twice. Obviously the repetition of the past can only eventuate in the repetition of the present. And that is precisely what education sets itself to counteract. The materialist forgets three outstanding and obvious facts. Firstly, science cannot be the whole of knowledge, because " science " (in his limited sense of the term) deals only with what appears. Secondly, power of insight depends not so much upon the senses as on moral qualities, the sense of sympathy and of fairness; it needs self-discipline as well as knowledge both of oneself and one's fellow-man. "How can a man," says Carlyle, "without clear vision in his heart first of all, have any clear vision in the head?" "Eyes and ears," said the ancient philosopher, "are bad witnesses for such as have barbarian souls." Thirdly, the tragedy of the past generation was not its failure to accumulate wealth; in that respect it was more successful than any generation which preceded it. The tragedy of the nineteenth century was that, when it had acquired wealth, it had no clear idea, either individually or collectively, what to do with it.

And yet the house of humanity faces both ways; it looks out towards the world of appearances as well as to the world of spirit, and is, in fact, the meeting-place of both. Materialism is not wrong because it deals with material things. It is wrong because it deals with nothing else. It is wrong, also, in education because taking the point of view of the adult, it makes the material product itself the all-important thing. In every right conception of education the child is central. The child is interested in things. It wants first to *sense* them, or as Froebel would say "to make the outer inner"; it wants to play with them, to construct with them, and along the line of this inward propulsion the educational process has to act. The "thing-studies" if one may so term them, which have been introduced into the curriculum, such as gardening, manual training (with cardboard, wood, metal), cooking, painting, modelling, games and dramatisation, are it is true later introductions, adopted mainly from utilitarian motive; and they have been ingrafted on the original trunk, being at first regarded as detachable extras, but they quickly showed that they were an organic part of the real educative process; they have already reacted on the other subjects of the curriculum, and have, in the earlier stages of education become central. In the same way, vocation is having great influence upon the higher terminal stages of education. All this is part of the most important of all correlations, the correlation of school with life.

But the child's interest in things is social. Through the primitive occupations of mankind, he is entering step by step into the heritage of the race, and into a richer fuller personal experience. The science which enlists a child's interest is not that which is presented from the logical, abstract point of view. The way in which the child acquires it is the same as that in which mankind acquired it—his occupation presents certain difficulties, to overcome these difficulties he has to exercise his thought, he invents and experiments; and so thought reacts upon occupation, occupation reacts upon thought. And out of that reciprocal action science is born. In the same way his play is social—in his games too he enters into the heritage of the race, and in playing them he is learning unconsciously the greatest of all arts, the art of living with others. In his play as well as in his school work the lines of his natural development show how he can be trained to co-operate with the law of human progress.

This fitness and readiness to co-operate with the great movement of human progress, all-round fitness of body, mind and spirit, provides the formula which fuses and reconciles two growing tendencies in modern education.

There is in the first place the movement towards self-expression and self-development—postulating for the scholar a larger measure of liberty in thought and action, and self-direction than hitherto—this movement is represented mainly by Dr Montessori, and by "What is and what might be"; it is a movement which is spreading upwards from the infant school to the higher standards. Side by side with it is the movement towards the fuller development of corporate life in the school, the movement which trains the child to put the school first in his thoughts, to live for the society to which he belongs and find his own personal well-being in the well-being of that society. This has been, ever since Arnold, sedulously fostered in the games of the public schools, and fruitful of good results in that limited sphere; it has been applied with conspicuous success to the development of self-government, and it has reached its fullest expression in the little Commonwealth of Mr Homer Lane. But we are beginning to recognise its wider applications, it is capable of transforming the spirit of the class-room activities as well as the activities of a playing field, it is in every way as applicable to the elementary school as to Eton, or Rugby, or Harrow, and to girls as well as to boys.

These two movements towards a fuller liberty of self-fulfilment, and towards a fuller and stronger social life, are convergent, and supplement, or rather complement, each other. Personality, after all, is best defined as "capacity for fellowship," and only in the social milieu can the individual find his real self-fulfilling. Unless he functions socially, the individual develops into eccentricity, negative criticism, and the cynical aloofness of the "superior person." On the other hand without freedom of individual develop-ment, the organisation of life becomes the death of the soul. Prussia has shown how the psychology of the crowd can be skilfully manipulated for the most sinister ends. It is a happy omen for our democracy that both these complementary movements are com-bined in the new life of the schools. To both appeals, the appeal of personal freedom, and the appeal of the corporate life, the British child is peculiarly responsive. Round these two health-centres the form of the new system will take shape and grow.

And growth it must be, not building. The body is not built up on the skeleton, the skeleton is secreted by the growing body. The hope of education is in the living principle of hope and enthusiasm, which stretches out towards perfection. One distrusts instinctively at the present time anything schematic. There are men, able enough as organisers, who will be ready to sit down and produce at two days' notice a full cut-and-dried scheme of educational reconstruction. They will take our present resources, and make the best of them, no doubt, re-arranging and re-manipulating them, and making them go as far as they can. They will shape the whole thing out in wood, and the result will be wooden. It will be static and stratified, with no upward lift. But that is not the way. Education is a thing of the spirit, it is instinct with life, θερμόν τι πρᾶγμα, as Aristotle would say, drawing upon resources that are not its own, "unseen yet crescive in its faculty" and in its growth taking to itself such outward form as it needs for the purpose of its inward life. Six years at least it will take for the new spirit to work itself out into the definite larger forms.

That does not mean that it will come without hard purposeful thinking and much patient effort. Education does not "happen" any more than "art happens," —and just as with the arts of the middle ages, so the well-being of education depends not on the chance appearance of a few men of genius but on the right training and love of the ordinary workman for his work. Education is a spiritual endeavour, and it will come, as the things of the spirit come, through patience in well-doing, through concentration of purpose on the highest, through drawing continually on the inexhaustible resources of the spiritual world. The supreme "maker" is the poet, the man of vision. For the administrator, the task is different from what it has been. It is for him to watch and help experiments, to prevent the abuse of freedom, not to preserve uniformities but to select variations. But he is handling a power which, as George Meredith says, "is a heaven-sent steeplechaser, and takes a flying leap of the ordinary barriers."

To-morrow is the day of opportunity. To-day is the day of preparation. Yesterday's ideals have become the practical politics of the present hour. Our countrymen recognise now as they have never done before that the problem of national reconstruction is in the main a problem of national education: "the future welfare of the nation," to use Mr Fisher's words, "depends upon its schools." Men make light now of the extra millions which a few years ago seemed to bar the way of progress. At the same time the discipline of the last three years has hammered into us a new consciousness of national solidarity and social obligation. As the whole energies of a united people are at this moment concentrated on the duty of destruction which is laid upon us, so after the war with no less urgency and no less oneness of heart the whole energies of a united nation must be concentrated on the upbuilding of life. That upbuilding is to be economic as well as spiritual, but those who think out most deeply the need of the economic situation, are most surely convinced that the problems of industry and commerce are at the bottom human problems and cannot find solution without a new sense of "co-operation and brotherliness[1]."

Such is the need and such the task. England is looking to her schools as she never did before. The aim of her education must be both high and wide, higher than lucre, wider than the nation. And the aim of our education cannot be fulfilled until the education of other peoples is infused with the same spirit. Education, like finance, must be planned on international lines by international consensus with a view to world peace. Only so can it fulfil the ultimate end which already looms on the horizon,

> Becoming when the time has birth
> A lever to uplift the earth
> And roll it on another course.

[1] Mr Angus Watson in *Eclipse or Empire*, p. 88.

II

THE TRAINING OF THE REASON

By W. R. INGE
Dean of St Paul's

The ideal object of education is that we should learn all that it concerns us to know, in order that thereby we may become all that it concerns us to be. In other words, the aim of education is the knowledge not of facts but of values. Values are facts apprehended in their relation to each other, and to ourselves. The wise man is he who knows the relative values of things. In this knowledge, and in the use made of it, is summed up the whole conduct of life. What are the things which are best worth winning for their own sakes, and what price must I pay to win them? And what are the things which, since I cannot have everything, I must be content to let go? How can I best choose among the various subjects of human interest, and the various objects of human endeavour, so that my activities may help and not hinder each other, and that my life may have a unity, or at least a centre round which my subordinate activities may be grouped. These are the chief questions which a man would ask, who desired to plan his life on rational principles, and whom circumstances allowed to choose his occupation.

He would desire to know himself, and to know the world, in order to give and receive the best value for his sojourn in it.

We English for the most part accept this view of education, and we add that the experience of life, or what we call knowledge of the world, is the best school of practical wisdom. We do not however identify practical wisdom with the life of reason but with that empirical substitute for it which we call common sense. There is in all classes a deep distrust of ideas, often amounting to what Plato called *misologia*, "hatred of reason." An Englishman, as Bishop Creighton said, not only has no ideas; he hates an idea when he meets one. We discount the opinion of one who bases his judgment on first principles. We think that we have observed that in high politics, for example, the only irreparable mistakes are those which are made by logical intellectualists. We would rather trust our fortunes to an honest opportunist, who sees by a kind of intuition what is the next step to be taken, and cares for no logic except the logic of facts. Reason, as Aristotle says, "moves nothing"; it can analyse and synthesise given data, but only after isolating them from the living stream of time and change. It turns a concrete situation into lifeless abstractions, and juggles with counters when it should be observing realities. Our prejudices against logic as a principle of conduct have been fortified by our national experience. We are not a quick-witted race; and we have succeeded where others have failed by dint of a kind of instinct for improvising the right course of action, a gift which is mainly the result of certain elementary virtues which we practise without thinking about them, justice, tolerance, and moderation. These qualities have, we think and think truly, been often wanting in the Latin nations, which pride themselves on lucidity of intellect and logical consistency in obedience to general principles. Recent philosophy has encouraged these advocates of common sense, who have long been "pragmatists" without knowing it, to profess their faith without shame. Intellect has been disparaged and instinct has been exalted. Intuition is a safer guide than reason, we are told; for intuition goes straight to the heart of a situation and has already acted while reason is debating. Much of this new philosophy is a kind of higher obscurantism; the man in the street applauds Bergson and William James because he dislikes science and logic, and values will, courage and sentiment. He used to be fond of repeating that Waterloo was won on the playing fields of our public schools, until it was painfully obvious that Colenso and Spion Kop were lost in the same place. We have muddled through so often that we have come half to believe in a providence which watches over unintelligent virtue. "Be good, sweet maid, and let who will be clever," we have said to Britannia. So we have acquiesced in being the worst educated people west of the Slav frontier.

I do not wish to dwell on the disadvantages which we have thus incurred in international competition—our inferiority to Germany in chemistry, and to almost every continental nation in scientific agriculture. This lesson we are learning, and are not likely to forget. It is our spiritual loss which we need to realise more fully. In the first place, the majority of Englishmen have no thought-out purpose in life beyond the call of "duty," which is an empty ideal until we know what our duty is. Confusion of means and ends is especially common in this country, though it is certainly to be found everywhere. The passion for irrational accumulation is one example of the error, which causes the gravest social inconvenience. The largest part of social injustice and suffering is caused by the unchecked indulgence of the acquisitive instinct by those who have the opportunity of indulging it, and who have formed a blind habit of indulging it. No one, however selfish, who had formed any reasonable estimate of the relative values of life, would devote his whole time to the economical exploitation of his neighbours, in order to pile up the instruments of a fuller life, which he will never use. To regard business as a kind of game is, from the highest point of view, right, and our nation gains greatly by applying the ethics of sport to all our external activities; but we err in living for our games, whether they happen to be commerce or football. A friend of mine expostulated with a Yorkshire manufacturer who was spending his old age in unnecessary toil for the benefit of a spendthrift heir. The old man answered, "If it gives him half as much pleasure to spend my half million as it has given me to make it, I don't grudge it him." That is not the spirit of the real miser or Mammon-worshipper. It is the spirit of a natural idealist who from want of education has no rational standard of good.   When such a man intervenes in educational matters, he is sure to take the standpoint of the so-called practical man, because he is blind to the higher values of life.   He will wish to make knowledge and wisdom instruments for the production of wealth, or the improvement of the material condition of the poor.   But knowledge and wisdom refuse to be so treated.   Like goodness and beauty, wisdom is one of the absolute values, the divine ideas.   As one of the Cambridge Platonists said, we must not make our intellectual faculties Gibeonites, hewers of wood and drawers of water to the will and affections. Wisdom must be sought for its own sake or we shall not find it.   Another effect of our *misologia* is the degradation of reasonable sympathy into sentimentalism, which regards pain as the worst of evils, and endeavours always to remove the effects of folly and wrong-doing, without investigating the causes.   That such sentimentalism is often kind only to be cruel, and that it frequently robs honest Peter to pay dishonest Paul, needs no demonstration.   Sentimentalism does not believe that prevention is better than cure, and practical politicians know too well that a scientific treatment of social maladies is out of the question in this country.   Others become fanatics, that is to say, worldlings who are too narrow and violent to understand the world.   The root of the evil is that a whole range of the higher values is inaccessible to the majority, because they know nothing of intellectual wealth.   And yet the real wealth of a nation consists in its imponderable possessions—in those things wherein one man's gain is not another man's loss, and which are not proved incapable of increase by any laws of thermo-dynamics. An inexhaustible treasure is freely open to all who have passed through a good course of mental training, a treasure which we can make our own according to our capacities, and our share of which we would not barter for any goods which the law of the land can give or take away. "The intelligent man," says Plato, "will prize those studies which result in his soul getting soberness, righteousness and wisdom, and will less value the others." The studies which have this effect are those which teach us to admire and understand the good, the true and the beautiful. They are, may we not say, humanism and science, pursued in a spirit of "admiration, hope and love." The trained reason is disinterested and fearless. It is not afraid of public opinion, because it "counts it a small thing that it should be judged by man's judgment"; its interests are so much wider than the incidents of a private career that base self-centred indulgence and selfish ambition are impossible to it. It is saved from pettiness, from ignorance, and from bigotry. It will not fall a victim to those undisciplined and disproportioned enthusiasms which we call fads, and which are a peculiar feature of English and North American civilisation. Such reforms as are carried out in this country are usually effected not by the reason of the many, but by the fanaticism of the few. A just balance may on the whole be preserved, but there is not much balance in the judgments of individuals.

Matthew Arnold, whose exhortations to his countrymen now seem almost prophetic, drew a strong contrast between the intellectual frivolity, or rather insensibility, of his countrymen and the earnestness of the Germans. He saw that England was saved a hundred years ago by the high spirit and proud resolution of a real aristocracy, which nevertheless was, like all aristocracies, "destitute of ideas." Our great families, he shows, could no longer save us, even if they had retained their influence, because power is now conferred by disciplined knowledge and applied science. It is the same warning which George Meredith reiterated with increasing earnestness in his later poems. What England needs, he says, is "brain."

> Warn her, Bard, that Power is pressing
>   Hotly for his dues this hour,
> Tell her that no drunken blessing
>   Stops the onward march of Power.
> Has she ears to take forewarnings,
>   She will cleanse her of her stains,
> Feed and speed for braver mornings
>   Valorously the growth of brains.
> Power, the hard man knit for action
>   Reads each nation on the brow;
> Cripple, fool, and petrifaction
>   Fall to him—are falling now.

And again:

> She impious to the Lord of hosts
> The valour of her off-spring boasts,
> Mindless that now on land and main
> His heeded prayer is active brain.

These faithful prophets were not heeded, and we have had to learn our lesson in the school of experience. She is a good teacher but her fees are very high.

The author of *Friendship's Garland* ended with a despairing appeal to the democracy, when his jeremiads evoked no response from the upper class, whom he called barbarians, or from the middle class, whom he regarded as incurably vulgar. The middle classes are apt to receive hard measure; they have few friends and many critics. We must go back to Euripides to find the bold statement that they are the best part of the community and "the salvation of the State"; but it is, on the whole, true. And our middle class is only superficially vulgar. Vulgarity, as Mr Robert Bridges has lately said, "is blindness to values; it is spiritual death." The middle class in Matthew Arnold's time was no doubt deplorably blind to artistic values; its productions survive to convict it of what he called Philistinism; but it is no longer devoid of taste or indifferent to beauty. And it has never been a contemptible artist in life. Mr Bridges describes the progress of vulgarity as an inverted Platonic progress. We descend, he says, from ugly forms to ugly conduct, and from ugly conduct to ugly principles, till we finally arrive at the absolute ugliness which is vulgarity. This identification of insensibility to beauty with moral baseness was something of a paradox even in Greece, and does not fit the English character at all. Our towns are ugly enough; our public buildings rouse no enthusiasm; and many of our monuments and stained glass windows seem to shout for a friendly Zeppelin to obliterate them. But we British have not descended to ugly conduct. Pericles and Plato would have found the bearing of this people in its supreme trial more "beautiful" than the Parthenon itself. The nation has shaken off its vulgarity even more easily and completely than its slackness and self-indulgence. We have borne ourselves with a courage, restraint, and dignity which, a Greek would say, could have only been expected of philosophers. And we certainly are not a nation of philosophers. We must not then be too hasty in calling all contempt for intellect vulgar. We have sinned by undervaluing the life of reason; but we are not really a vulgar people. Our secular faith, the real religion of the average Englishman, has its centre in the idea of a gentleman, which has of course no essential connection with heraldry or property in land. The upper classes, who live by it, are not vulgar, in spite of the absence of ideas with which Matthew Arnold twits them; the middle classes who also respect this ideal, are further protected by sound moral traditions; and the lower classes have a cheery sense of humour which is a great antiseptic against vulgarity. But though the Poet Laureate has not, in my opinion, hit the mark in calling vulgarity our national sin, he has done well in calling attention to the danger which may beset educational reform from what we may call democratism, the tendency to level down all superiorities in the name ot equality and good fellowship. It is the opposite fault to the aristocraticism which beyond all else led to the decline of Greek culture—

the assumption that the lower classes must remain excluded from intellectual and even from moral excellence. With us there is a tendency to condemn ideals of self-culture which can be called "aristocratic." But we need specialists in this as in every other field, and the populace must learn that there is such a thing as real superiority, which has the right and duty to claim a scope for its full exercise.

The fashionable disparagement of reason, and exaltation of will, feeling or instinct would be more dangerous in a less scientific age. The Italian metaphysician Aliotta has lately brought together in one survey the numerous leaders in the great "reaction against science," and they are a formidable band. Pragmatists, voluntarists, activists, subjective idealists, emotional mystics, and religious conservatives, have all joined in assaulting the fortress of science which half a century ago seemed impregnable. But the besieged garrison continues to use its own methods and to trust in its own hypotheses; and the results justify the confidence with which the assaults of the philosophers are ignored. We are told that the scientific method is ultimately appropriate only to the abstractions of mathematics. But nature herself seems to have a taste for mathematical methods. A sane idealism believes that the eternal verities are adumbrated, not travestied, in the phenomenal world, and does not forget how much of what we call observation of nature is demonstrably the work of mind. The world as known to science is itself a spiritual world, from which certain valuations are, for special purposes, excluded. To deny the authority of the discursive reason, which has its proper province in this sphere, is to destroy the possibility of all knowledge. Nor can we, without loss and danger, exalt instinct or intuition above reason. Instinct is a faculty which belongs to unprogressive species. It is necessarily unadaptable and unable to deal with any new situation. Consecrated custom may keep Chinese civilisation safe in a state of torpid immobility for five thousand years; but fifty years of Europe will achieve more, and will at last present Cathay with the alternative of moving on or moving off. Instinct might lead us on if progress were an automatic law of nature, but this belief, though widely held, is sheer superstition.

We have to convert the public mind in this country to faith in trained and disciplined reason. We have to convince our fellow-citizens not only that the duty of self-preservation requires us to be mentally as well equipped as the French, Germans and Americans, but that a trained intelligence is in itself "more precious than rubies." Blake said that "a fool shall never get to Heaven, be he never so holy." It is at any rate true that ignorance misses the best things in this life. If Englishmen would only believe this, the whole spirit of our education would be changed, which is much more important than to change the subjects taught. It does not matter very much what is taught; the important question to ask is what is learnt. This is why the controversy about religious education was mainly fatuous. The "religious lesson" can hardly ever make a child religious; religion, in point of fact, is seldom taught at all; it is caught, by contact with someone who has it. Other subjects can be taught and can be learnt; but the teaching will be stiff collar-work, and the learning evanescent, if the pupil is not interested in the subject. And how little encouragement the average boy gets at home to train his reason and form intellectual tastes! He may probably be exhorted to "do well in his examination," which means that he is to swallow carefully prepared gobbets of crude information, to be presently disgorged in the same state. The examination system flourishes best where there is no genuine desire for mental cultivation. If there were any widespread enthusiasm for knowledge as an integral part of life the revolt against this mechanical and commercialised system of testing results would be universal. As things are, a clever boy trains for an examination as he trains for a race; and goes out of training as fast as possible when it is over. Meanwhile the romance of his life is centred in those more generous and less individual competitions in the green fields, which our schools and universities have developed to such perfection. In classes which have small opportunities for physical exercises, vicarious athletics, with not a little betting, are a disastrous substitute. But the soul is dyed the colour of its leisure thoughts. "As a man thinketh in his heart, so is he." This is why no change in the curriculum can do much for education, as long as the pupils imbibe no respect for intellectual values at home, and find none among their school-fellows. And yet the capacity for real intellectual interest is only latent in most boys. It can be kindled in a whole class by a master who really loves and believes in his subject. Some of the best public school teachers in the last century were hot-tempered men whose disciplinary performances were ludicrous. But they were enthusiastic humanists, and keen scholars passed year by year out of their class-rooms.

The importance of a good curriculum is often exaggerated. But a bad selection of subjects, and a bad method of teaching them, may condemn even the best teacher to ineffectiveness. Nothing, for example, can well be more unintelligent than the manner of teaching the classics in our public schools. The portions of Greek and Latin authors construed during a lesson are so short that the boys can get no idea of the book as a whole; long before they finish it they are moved up into another form. And over all the teaching hangs the menace of the impending examination, the riddling Sphinx which, as Seeley said in a telling quotation from Sophocles, forces us to attend to what is at our feet, neglecting all else—all the imponderables in which the true value of education consists. The tyranny of examinations has an important influence upon the choice of subjects as well as upon the manner of teaching them; for some subjects, which are remarkably stimulating to the mind of the pupil, are neglected, because they are not well adapted for examinations. Among these, unfortunately, are our own literature and language.

It is therefore necessary, even in a short essay

which professes to deal only with generalities, to make some suggestions as to the main subjects which our education should include. As has been indicated already, I would divide them into main classes— science and humanism. Every boy should be instructed in both branches up to a certain point. We must firmly resist those who wish to make education purely scientific, those who, in Bacon's words, "call upon men to sell their books and build furnaces, quitting and forsaking Minerva and the Muses and relying upon Vulcan." We want no young specialists of twelve years old; and a youth without a tincture of humanism can never become

A man foursquare, withouten flaw ywrought.

Of the teaching of science I am not competent to speak. But as an instrument of mind-training, and even of liberal education, it seems to me to have a far higher value than is usually conceded to it by humanists. To direct the imagination to the infinitely great and the infinitely small, to vistas of time in which a thousand years are as one day; to the tremendous forces imprisoned in minute particles of matter; to the amazing complexity of the mechanism by which the organs of the human body perform their work; to analyse the light which has travelled for centuries from some distant star; to retrace the history of the earth and the evolution of its inhabitants—such studies cannot fail to elevate the mind, and only prejudice will disparage them. They promote also a fine respect for truth and fact, for order and outline, as the Greeks said, with a wholesome dislike of sophistry and rhetoric. The air which blows about scientific studies is like the air of a mountain top—thin, but pure and bracing. And as a subject of education science has a further advantage which can hardly be over-estimated. It is in science that most of the new dis-coveries are being made. "The rapture of the forward view" belongs to science more than to any other study. We may take it as a well-established principle in education that the most advanced teachers should be researchers and discoverers as well as lecturers, and that the rank and file should be learners as well as instructors. There is no subject in which this ideal is so nearly attainable as in science.

And yet science, even for its own sake, must not claim to occupy the whole of education. The mere *Naturforscher* is apt to be a poor philosopher himself, and his pupils may turn out very poor philosophers indeed. The laws of psychical and spiritual life are not the same as the laws of chemistry or biology; and the besetting sin of the scientist is to try to explain everything in terms of its origin instead of in terms of its full development: "by their roots," he says, "and not by their fruits, ye shall know them." This is a contradiction of Aristotle (ἡ φύσις τέλος ἐστίν), and of a greater than Aristotle. The training of the reason must include the study of the human mind, "the throne of the Deity," in its most characteristic pro-ducts. Besides science, we must have humanism, as the other main branch of our curriculum.

The advocates of the old classical education have been gallantly fighting a losing battle for over half a century; they are now preparing to accept inevitable defeat. But their cause is not lost, if they will face the situation fairly. It is only lost if they persist in identifying classical education with linguistic proficiency. The study of foreign languages is a fairly good mental discipline for the majority; for the minority it may be either more or less than a fair discipline. But only a small fraction of mankind is capable of enthusiasm for language, for its own sake. The art of expressing ideas in appropriate and beautiful forms is one of the noblest of human achievements, and the two classical languages contain many of the finest examples of good writing that humanity has produced. But the average boy is incapable of appreciating these values, and the waste of time which might have been profitably spent is, under our present system, most deplorable. It may also be maintained that the conscientious editor and the conscientious tutor have between them ruined the classics as a mental discipline. Fifty years ago, English commentatorship was so poor that the pupil had to use his wits in reading the classics; now if one goes into an undergraduate's room, one finds him reading the text with the help of a translation, two editions with notes, and a lecture note-book. No faculty is being used except the memory, which Bishop Creighton calls "the most worthless of our mental powers." The practice of prose and verse composition, often ignorantly decried, has far more educational value; but it belongs to the linguistic art which, if we are right, is not to be demanded of all students. Are we then to restrict the study of the classics to those who have a pretty taste for style? If so, the cause of classical education is indeed lost. But I can see no reason why some of the great Greek and Latin authors should not be read, *in translations*, as part of the normal training in history, philosophy and literature. I am well aware of the loss which a great author necessarily suffers by translation; but I have no hesitation in saying that the average boy would learn far more of Greek literature, and would imbibe far more of the Greek spirit, by reading the whole of Herodotus, Thucydides, the *Republic* of Plato, and some of the plays in good translations, than he now acquires by going through the classical mill at a public school. The classics, like almost all other literature, must be read in masses to be appreciated. Boys think them dull mainly because of the absurd way in which they are made to study them.

I shall not make any ambitious attempt to sketch out a scheme of literary studies. My subject is the training of the reason. But two principles seem to me to be of primary importance. The first is that we should study the psychology of the developing reason at different ages, and adapt our method of teaching accordingly. The memory is at its best from the age of ten to fifteen, or thereabouts. Facts and dates, and even long pieces of poetry, which have been committed to memory in early boyhood, remain with us as a possession for life. We would most of us give a great deal in middle age to recover that astonishingly retentive memory which we possessed as little boys.

On the other hand, ratiocination at that age is difficult and irksome. A young boy would rather learn twenty rules than apply one principle. Accordingly the first years of boyhood are the time for learning by heart. Quantities of good poetry, and useful facts of all kinds should be entrusted to the boy's memory to keep: it will assimilate them readily, and without any mental overstrain. But eight or ten years later, "cramming" is injurious both to the health and to the intellect. Years have brought, if not the philosophic mind, yet at any rate a mind which can think and argue. The memory is weaker and the process of loading it with facts is more unpleasant. At this stage the whole system of teaching should be different. One great evil of examinations is that they prolong the stage of mere memorising to an age at which it is not only useless but hurtful. Another valuable guide is furnished by observing what authors the intelligent boy likes and dislikes. His taste ought certainly to be consulted, if our main object is to interest him in the things of the mind. The average intelligent boy likes Homer and does not like Virgil; he is interested by Tacitus and bored by Cicero; he loves Shakespeare and revels in Macaulay, who has a special affinity for the eternal schoolboy.

My other principle is that since we are training young Englishmen, whom we hope to turn into true and loyal citizens, we shall presumably find them most responsive to the language, literature, and history of their own country. This would be a commonplace, not worth uttering, in any other country; in England it is, unfortunately, far from being generally accepted. Nothing sets in a stronger light the inertia and thought-lessness, not to say stupidity, of the British character, in all matters outside the domain of material and moral interests, than our neglect of the magnificent spiritual heritage which we possess in our own history and literature. Wordsworth, in one of those noble sonnets which are now, we are glad to hear, being read by thousands in the trenches and by myriads at home, proclaims his faith in the victory of his country over Napoleon because he thinks of her glorious past.

> We must be free or die, who speak the tongue
> That Shakespeare spake, the faith and morals hold
> That Milton held. In everything we are sprung
> Of Earth's best blood, have titles manifold.

It is a high boast, but it is true. But what have we done to fire the imagination of our boys and girls with the vision of our great and ancient nation, now struggling for its existence? What have we taught them of Shakespeare and Milton, of Elizabeth and Cromwell, of Nelson and Wellington? Have we even tried to make them understand that they are called to be the temporary custodians of very glorious traditions, and the trustees of a spiritual wealth compared with which the gold mines of the Rand are but dross? Do we even teach them, in any rational manner, the fine old language which has been slowly perfected for centuries, and which is now being used up and debased by the rubbishy newspapers which form almost the sole reading of the majority? We have marvelled at the slowness with which the masses realised that the

country was in danger, and at the stubbornness with
which some of the working class clung to their sectional
interests and ambitions when the very life of England
was at stake. In France the whole people saw at
once what was upon them; the single word *patrie*
was enough to unite them in a common enthusiasm
and stern determination. With us it was hardly so;
many good judges think that but for the " Lusitania "
outrage and the Zeppelins, part of the population
would have been half-hearted about the war, and we
should have failed to give adequate support to our
allies. The cause is not selfishness but ignorance and
want of imagination; and what have we done to tap
the sources of an intelligent patriotism? We are being
saved not by the reasoned conviction of the populace,
but by its native pugnacity and bull-dog courage.
This is not the place to go into details about English
studies; but can anyone doubt that they could be
made the basis of a far better education than we now
give in our schools? We have especially to remember
that there is a real danger of the modern Englishman
being cut off from the living past. Scientific studies
include the earlier phases of the earth, but not the
past of the human race and the British people. Christianity has been a valuable educator in this way,
especially when it includes an intelligent knowledge
of the Bible. But the secular education of the masses
is now so much severed from the stream of tradition
and sentiment which unites us with the older civilisations, that the very language of the Churches is becoming unintelligible to them, and the influence of

organised religion touches only a dwindling minority. And yet the past lives in us all; lives inevitably in its dangers, which the accumulated experience of civilisation, valued so slightly by us on its spiritual side, can alone help us to surmount. A nation, like an individual, must "wish his days to be bound each to each by natural piety." It too must strive to keep its memory green, to remember the days of old and the years that are past. The Jews have always had, in their sacred books, a magnificent embodiment of the spirit of their race; and who can say how much of their incomparable tenacity and ineradicable hopefulness has been due to the education thus imparted to every Jewish child? We need a Bible of the English race, which shall be hardly less sacred to each succeeding generation of young Britons than the Old Testament is to the Jews. England ought to be, and may be, the spiritual home of one quarter of the human race, for ages after our task as a world-power shall have been brought to a successful issue, and after we in this little island have accepted the position of mother to nations greater than ourselves. But England's future is precious only to those to whom her past is dear.

I am not suggesting that the history and literatures of other countries should be neglected, or that foreign languages should form no part of education. But the main object is to turn out good Englishmen, who may continue worthily and even develop further a glorious national tradition. To do this, we must appeal constantly to the imagination, which

Wordsworth has boldly called "reason in her most exalted mood." We may thus bring a little poetry and romance into the monotonous lives of our hand-workers. It may well be that their discontent has more to do with the starving of their spiritual nature than we suppose. For the intellectual life, like divine philosophy, is not dull and crabbed, as fools suppose, but musical as is Apollo's lute.

Can we end with a definition of the happiness and well-being, which is the goal of education, as of all else that we try to do? Probably we cannot do better than accept the famous definition of Aristotle, which however we must be careful to translate rightly. "Happiness, or well-being, is an activity of the soul directed towards excellence, in an unhampered life." Happiness consists in doing rather than being; the activity must be that of the soul—the whole man acting as a person; it must be directed towards excellence—not exclusively moral virtue, but the best work that we can do, of whatever kind; and it must be unhampered—we must be given the opportunity of doing the best that is in us to do. To awaken the soul; to hold up before it the images of whatsoever things are true, lovely, noble, pure, and of good report; and to remove the obstacles which stunt and cripple the mind; this is the work which we have called the Training of the Reason.

III

THE TRAINING OF THE IMAGINATION

By A. C. BENSON
Master of Magdalene College, Cambridge

It might be hastily assumed by a reader bent on critical consideration, that the subject of my essay had a certain levity or fancifulness about it. Works of imagination, as by a curious juxtaposition they are called, are apt to lie under an indefinable suspicion, as including unbusinesslike and romantic fictions, of which the clear-cut and well-balanced mind must beware, except for the sake, perhaps, of the frankest and least serious kind of recreation. Considering the part which the best and noblest works of imagination must always play in a literary education, it has often surprised me to reflect how little scope ordinary literary exercises give for the use of that particular faculty. The old themes and verses aimed at producing decorous centos culled from the works of classical rhetoricians and poets. No boy, at least in my day, was ever encouraged to take a line of his own, and to strike out freely across country in pursuit of imagined adventures. Even English teaching in its earlier stages seldom aimed at more than transcriptions of actual experience, a day spent in the country, or a walk beside the sea. Only quite recently have boys and girls been encouraged to write poems and stories out of their own imaginations; and even now there are plenty of educational critics who would consider such exercises as dilettante things lacking in practical solidity.

But I desire in this essay to go further back into the roots of the subject, and my first position is plainly this; that imagination, pure and simple, is a common enough faculty; not perhaps the creative imagination which can array scenes of life, construct romantic experiences, and embody imaginary characters in dramatic situations, but the much simpler sort of imagination which takes pleasure in recalling past memories, and in forecasting and anticipating interesting events. The boy who, weary of the school-term, considers what he will do on the first day of the holidays, or who anxiously forebodes paternal displeasure, is exercising his imagination; and the truth is that the faculty of imagination plays an immense part in all human happiness and unhappiness, considering that, whenever we take refuge from the present in memories or in anticipations, we are using it. The first point then that I shall consider is whether this restless and influential faculty ought not in any case to be *trained*, so that it may not either be atrophied or become over-dominant; and the second point will be the further consideration as to whether the faculty of creative imagination is a thing which should be deliberately developed.

In the first place then, it seems to me simply

extraordinary that so little heed is paid in education
to the using and controlling of what is one of the most
potent instinctive forces of the mind. We take careful thought how to strengthen and fortify the body,
we go on to spending many hours upon putting
memory through its paces, and in developing the
reason and the intelligence; we pass on from that to
exercising and purifying the character and the will;
we try to make vice detestable and virtue desirable.
But meanwhile, what is the little mind doing? It
submits to the drudgery imposed upon it, it accom-
modates itself more or less to the conditions of its
life; it learns a certain conduct and demeanour for
use in public. Yet all the time the thought of the
boy is running backwards and forwards in secrecy,
considering the memories of its experience, pleasant
or unpleasant, and comforting itself in tedious hours
by framing little plans for the future. I remember
my old schoolmastering days, and the hours I spent
with a class of boys sitting in front of me; how constantly one saw boys in the midst of their work, with
pen suspended and page unturned, look up with that
expression denoting that some vision had passed before the inward eye—which, as Wordsworth justly
observes, constitutes "the bliss of solitude"—oblit-
erating for a moment the surrounding scene. I do
not mean that the thought was a distant or an exalted
one—probably it was some entirely trivial remi-
niscence, or the anticipation of some coming amusement. But I do not think I exaggerate when I say
that probably the greater part of a human being's

unoccupied hours, and probably a considerable part of the hours supposed to be occupied, are spent in some similar exercise of the imagination. What a confirmation of this is to be found in the phenomena of sleep and dreams! Then the instinct is steadily at work, neither remembering nor anticipating, but weaving together the results of experience into a self-taught tale.

And then if one considers later life, it is no exaggeration to say that the greater part of human happiness and unhappiness consists in the dwelling upon what has been, what may be, what might be, and, alas, in our worst moments, upon what might have been "My unhappiest experiences," said Lord Beaconsfield, "have been those which never happened"; and again the same acute critic of life said that half the clever people he knew were under the impression that they were hated and envied, the other half that they were admired and loved;—and that neither were right!

The imaginative faculty then is a species of self-representation, the power of considering our own life and position as from the outside; from it arise both the cheerful hopes and schemes of the sound mind, and the shadowy anxieties and fears of the mind which lacks robustness. It certainly does seem singular that this deep and persistent element in human life is left so untrained and unregarded, to range at will, to feed upon itself. All that the teacher does is to insist as far as possible on a certain concentration of the mind on business at particular times, and if he has ethical purposes at heart, he may sometimes speak to a boy on the advisability of not allowing his mind to dwell upon base or sensual thoughts; but how little attempt is ever made to train the mind in deliberate and continuous self-control!

The latest school of pathologists, in the treatment of obsessed or insane persons, pay very close attention to the subjects of their dreams, and attribute much nerve-misery to the atrophy, or suppression by circumstances, of instincts which betray themselves in dreams. I am inclined to think that the educators of the future must somehow contrive to do more—indeed they cannot well do less than is actually done—in teaching the control of that secret undercurrent of thought in which happiness and unhappiness really reside. Those who have lived much with boys will know what havoc suspense or disappointment or anxiety or sensuality or unpopularity can make in an immature character. It seems to me that we ought not to leave all this without guidance or direction, but to make a frontal attack upon it. I do not mean that it is necessary to probe too deeply into the imagination, but I believe that the subject should be frankly spoken about, and suggestions made. The point is to get the will to work, and to induce the mind, in the first place, to realise and practise its power of self-command; and in the second place, to show that it is possible to evict an unwholesome thought by the deliberate welcoming and entertaining of a wholesome one. The best of all cures is to provide every boy with some occupation which he indubitably loves. There are a good many boys whose work is not interesting to them, and a certain number to whom the prescribed games are a matter of routine rather than of active pleasure. Indeed it may be said that hardly any boys enjoy either work or games in which they see no possibility of any personal distinction. It is therefore of great importance that every boy whose chances of successful performance are small should be encouraged to have a definite hobby; for an occupation which the mind can remember with pleasure and anticipate with delight supplies the food for the restless imagination, which may otherwise become dreary from inaction, or tainted by thoughts of baser pleasure. A schoolmaster only salves his conscience by supplying a strict time-table and regular games. A house master ought to be most careful in the case of boys whose work is languid and proficiency in games small, to find out what the boy really likes and enjoys, and to encourage it by every means in his power. That is the best corrective, to administer wholesome food for the mind to digest. But I believe that good teachers ought to go much further, and speak quite plainly to boys, from time to time, on the necessity of practising control of thought. My own experience is that boys were always interested in any talk, call it ethical or religious, which based itself directly upon their own actual experience. I can conceive that a teacher who told a class to sit still for three minutes and think about anything they pleased, and added that he would then have something to tell them, might have an admirable object-lesson in getting them to consider how swift and far-ranging their fancies had been; or again he might practise them in concentration of thought by asking them to think for five minutes on a perfectly definite thing—to imagine themselves in a wood, or by the sea, or in a chemist's shop, let us say, and then getting them to put down on paper a list of definite objects which they had imagined. The process could be infinitely extended; but if it were done with some regularity, it would certainly be possible to train boys to concentrate themselves in reflection and recollected observation. Or again a quality might be propounded, such as generosity or spitefulness, and the boys required to construct an imaginary anecdote of the simplest kind to illustrate it. This would have the effect of training the mind at all events to focus itself, and this is just what drudgery pure and simple will not do. The aim is not to train mere memory or logical accuracy, but to strengthen that great faculty which we loosely call imagination, which is the power of evoking mental images, and of migrating from the present into the past or the future.

I believe it to be a very notable lack in our theory of education that so little attempt is made to bring the will to bear upon what may be called the sub-conscious mind. It is that strange undercurrent of thought which is so imprudently neglected, which throws up on its banks, without any apparent purpose or aim, the ideas and images which lurk within it. I do not say that such a training would immediately give self-control, but most peoples' worst sufferings are caused by what is called "having something on their mind"; and yet, so far as I know, in the process of education, no attempt whatever is made, except quite incidentally, to dispossess the strong man armed by the stronger victor, or to help immature minds to hold an unpleasant or a pleasant thought at arm's length, or to train them in the power of resolutely substituting a current of more wholesome images. The subconscious mind is too often treated as a thing beyond control, and yet the pathological power of suggestion, by which a thought is implanted like a seed in the mind, which presently appears to be rooted and flowering, ought to show us that we have within our reach an extraordinarily potent psychological implement.

So far then on the more negative side. I have indicated my strong belief that much may be done to train the mind in self-control. Indeed our whole education is built upon the faith that we can, perhaps not implant new faculties, but develop dormant ones; and I am persuaded that when future generations come to survey our methods and processes of education, they will regard with deep bewilderment the amazing fact that we applied so careful a training to other faculties, and yet left so helplessly alone the training of the imaginative faculty, upon which, as I have said, our happiness and unhappiness mainly depend. We must all of us be aware of the fact that there have been times in our lives when all was prosperous, and when we were yet overshadowed with dreary thoughts; or again times when in discomfort, or under the shadow of failure, or at critical or tragic moments, we have had an unreasonable alertness and cheerfulness. All that is due to the subconscious mind, and we ought at least to try experiments in making it obey us better.

I now pass on to consider a further possibility, and that is of training and developing a higher sort of creative imagination. It is all in reality part of the same subject, because it seems to be certain that most human beings suffer by the suppression or the dormancy of existing faculties. It is here, I believe, that much of our intellectual education fails, from the tendency to direct so much attention to purely logical and reasoning faculties, and to the resolute subtraction from education of pure and simple enjoyment. I used to try many experiments as a schoolmaster, and I remember at one time bribing a slow and unintelligent class into some sort of concentration by promising that I would tell a story for a few minutes at the end of school, if a bit of work had been satisfactorily mastered. It certainly produced a lot of cheerful effort; my story was simple enough, description as brief and vivid as I could make it, and brisk tangible incidents. But the silence, the luxurious abandonment of small minds to an older and more pictorial imagination, the dancing light in open eyes, did really give me for once a sense of power which I never had in teaching Latin Prose or the Greek conditional sentence. I always told stories for an hour on Sunday evenings to the boys in my house, and though few of my intellectual and ethical counsels are remembered by old pupils, I never met one who did not recollect the stories.

Now we have here, I believe, a source of intellectual pleasure which is consistently neglected and even despised. It is regarded as a mere luxury; but we do not make the mistake of substituting gymnastics for games, and removing the pleasure of personal performance. Why can we not also do something to encourage what old Hawtrey used so beautifully to call "the sweet pride of authorship"? The worst of it all is that we look so much to tangible results. I do not mean that we must try to develop Shakespeares, Shelleys, Thackerays; such airy creatures have a way of catering for themselves! I do not at all want to turn out a generation of third-rate writing amateurs. But many boys have a distinct pleasure not only in listening to imaginations, and riding like the beetle on the engine, but in evoking and realising some little vision and creation of their own brains. Of course there are boys to whom mental activity is all of the nature of a cross laid upon them for some purpose, wise or unwise. But there are also a good many shy boys, who will not venture to make themselves conspicuous by literary and imaginative feats, and who yet if it were a matter of course and wont, would throw themselves with intense pleasure into literary creation. The work done, for instance, at Shrewsbury, at the Perse School, at Carlisle Grammar School, in this direction—I daresay it is done elsewhere, but I have seen the work of these three schools with my own eyes—show what quite average boys are capable of in both English poetry and English prose.

One of the best points of such a system of literary composition is that even if slower boys cannot effect much, it gives a most wholesome opening to the creative faculties of boys, whose minds, if stifled and compressed, are most likely to work in unwholesome and tormenting directions.

My suggestion then becomes part of a larger plea, the plea for the more direct cultivation of enjoyment in education. Some of our worst mistakes in education arise from our not basing it upon the actual needs and faculties of human nature, but upon the supposed constitution of a child constructed by the starved imagination of pedants and moralists and practical men.

One of the first requisites in cultivating intellectual and artistic pleasure is to build up taste out of the actual perceptions of the child. That is a factor which has been most stubbornly and unintelligently disregarded in education. Developments in character are of the nature of living things; they cannot be superimposed; they must be rooted in the temperament, and they must draw nurture and sustenance out of the spirit, as the seed imbibes its substance from the unseen soil and the hidden waters. But what has been constantly done is to introduce the childish mind, only capable of appreciating the broadest effects and the simplest romance, directly and suddenly to the biggest masterpieces. The absence of all gradation and reconciliation has been

characteristic of our literary education. Of course
there is an initial difficulty in the case of the classics,
that there is very little in either Greek or Latin which
really appeals to an immature taste at all; and such
books as might appeal to inquisitive and inexperienced
minds, such as Homer or the *Anabasis* of Xenophon,
are made unattractive by the method of giving such
short snippets, and insisting on what used to be
called thorough parsing. Even *Alice in Wonderland*,
let me say, could only prove a drearily bewildering
book, if read at the rate of twenty lines a lesson, and
if the principal tenses of all the verbs had to be repeated correctly. It is absolutely essential, if any
love of literature is to be superinduced, that something
should be read fast enough to give some sense of
continuity and range and horizon. The practice of
dictionary-turning is sufficient by itself to destroy intellectual pleasure, but it used to be defended as a
base sort of bribe to strengthen memory: it was
argued that boys would try to remember words to
save themselves the trouble of looking them up. But
this has no origin in fact. Boys used not to be encouraged to guess at words, but to be punished for
shirking work if they had not looked them out. It is
to be hoped that English will be in the future increasingly taught in schools; but even so there is the
danger of connecting it too much with erudition.
The old *Clarendon Press Shakespeare* was an almost
perfect example of how not to edit Shakespeare for
boys; the introductions were learned and scholarly,
the notes were crammed with philology, derivation,

illustration. As a matter of fact there is a good deal that is interesting, even to small minds, in the connection and derivation of words, if briskly communicated. Most boys are responsive to the pleasure of finding a familiar word concealed under a variation of shape; but this should be conveyed orally. What is really requisite is that boys should be taught how to read a book intelligently. In dealing with classical books, vocabulary must be always a difficulty, and I myself very much doubt the advisability in the case of average boys of attempting to teach more than one foreign language at a time, especially when in dealing, say, with three kindred languages, such as Latin, French, and English, the same word, such as *spiritus*, *esprit*, and *spirit* bear very different significations. The great need is that there should be some work going on in which the boys should not be conscious of dragging an ever-increasing burden of memory. Let me take a concrete case. A poem like the *Morte d'Arthur*, or *The Lay of the Last Minstrel*, is well within the comprehension of quite small boys. These could be read in a class, after an introductory lecture as to date, scene, dramatis personae, with perfect ease, words explained as they occurred, difficult passages paraphrased, and the whole action of the story could pass rapidly before the eye. Most boys have a distinct pleasure in rhyme and metre. Of course it is an immense gain if the master can really read in a spirited and moving manner, and a training in reading aloud should form a part of every schoolmaster's outfit. I should wish to see this reading lesson a daily hour for all younger boys, so as to form a real basis of education. Three of these hours could be given to English, and three to French, for in French there is a wide range both of simple narrative stories and historical romances. The aim to be kept in view would be the very simple one of proving that interest, amusement and emotion can be derived from books which, unassisted, only boys of tougher intellectual fibre could be expected to attack. The personalities of the authors of these books should be carefully described, and the result of such reading, persevered in steadily, would be, what is one of the most stimulating rewards of wider knowledge, the sudden realisation, that is, that books and authors are not lonely and isolated phenomena, but that the literature of a nation is like a branching tree, all connected and intertwined, and that the books of a race mirror faithfully and vividly the ideas of the age out of which they sprang. What makes books dull is the absence of any knowledge by the reader of why the author was at the trouble of expressing himself in that particular way at that particular time. When, as a small boy, I read a book of which the whole genesis was obscure to me, it used to appear to me vaguely that it must have been as disagreeable to the author to write it as it was for me to read it. But if it can be once grasped that books are the outcome of a writer's interest or sense of beauty or emotion or joy, the whole matter wears a different aspect.

The same principle applies with just the same force to history and geography; both of these studies can be made interesting, if they are not regarded as isolated groups of phenomena, but are approached from the boy's own experience as opening away and outwards from what is going on about him. The object is or ought to be slowly to extend the boy's horizon, to show him that history holds the seeds and roots of the present, and that geography is the life-drama which he sees about him, enacting itself under different climatic and physiographical conditions. The dreariness and dreadfulness of knowledge to the immature mind is because it represents itself as a mass of dry facts to be mastered without having any visible or tangible connection with the boy's own experience. The aim should rather be to teach him to look with zest and interest at what is going on outside his own narrow circle, and to help him to move perceptively along the paths of time and space which diverge in all directions from the scene where he finds himself.

It may be indisputably stated that all connected knowledge is stimulating, and that all unconnected knowledge is at best mechanical. Perhaps one of the most fruitful of all subjects is vivid biography, and no serious educator could perform a more valuable task than in providing a series of biographies of great men, really intelligible to youthful minds. As a rule, biographies of the first order require an amount of detailed knowledge in the reader which puts them out of the reach of ill-stored minds. But I have again and again found with boys that simple biographical lectures are among the most attractive of all lessons.

At one time, with my private pupils, I would take a book at random out of my shelves, read an interesting extract or two, and then say that I would try to show why the author chose such a subject, why he wrote as he did, and how it all sprang out of his life and character and circumstances.

Of course the difficulty in all this is that the field of knowledge is so vast and various, while the capacities of boys are so small, and the time to be spent on their education so short, that we quail before the attempt to grapple with the problem. We have moreover a vague idea that the well-informed man ought to have a general notion of the world as it is, the course of history, the literature of the ages; and at the same time the scientists are maintaining that a general knowledge of the laws and processes of nature is even more urgently needed. I cannot treat of science here, but I fully subscribe to the belief that a general knowledge of science is essential. But the result of our believing that it is advisable to know so much, is that we attempt to spread the thinnest and driest paste of knowledge over the mind, and all the vivid life of it evaporates in the process. The thing is, frankly, far too big to attempt; and we must henceforth set our faces against the attainment of mere knowledge as either advisable or possible. What we must try to do is to educate the faculties of curiosity, interest, imagination and sympathy; we must begin from the boy himself, and conduct him away from himself. What we really ought to aim at is to give him the sense that he is surrounded by strange and beautiful mysteries of nature, of which he can himself observe certain phenomena; that human history, as well as the great world about him, is crowded with interesting and animating figures who have laboured, toiled, loved, acted, suffered, sinned, have felt the impulse both of base and selfish desires, but no less of beautiful, exalted, and inspiring hopes. We want to convince the young that it is not well to be narrow, close-fisted, insolent, suspicious, petty, self-satisfied. *Imaginative sympathy*, that is to be the end of all our efforts. If we aim only at producing sympathy, we may get a vague sentimentalism which is just distressed by apparent suffering, and anxious to relieve it momentarily, without reflecting whether it is not the outcome of perfectly curable faults of system and habit. If we aim only at imagination, then we get a barren artistic pleasure in dramatic situations and romantic effects. What we ought to aim at is the sympathy which pities and feels for others, as well as admires and imitates them; and this must be reinforced by the imagination which can concern itself with the causes of what otherwise are but vague emotions. We want to make boys on the one hand detest tyranny and high-handedness and bigotry and ruthless exercise of power, and on the other hand mistrust stupidity and ignorance and baseness and selfishness and suspiciousness. The study of high literature is valuable not as a mere exercise in erudition and linguistic nicety and critical taste, but because the great books mirror best the highest hopes and visions of human nature. The precise extent of the intellectual range matters very little, compared with the perceptiveness and emotion by which the realisation of other lives, other needs, other activities, other problems are accompanied.

I must not be supposed, in saying this, to be leaving out of sight the virile exercise of logical and rational faculties; but that is another side of education; and the grave deficiency which I detect in the old theory was that practically all the powers and devices of education were devoted to what was called fortifying the mind and making it into a perfect instrument, while there were left out of sight the motives which were to guide the use of that instrument, and the boy was led to suppose that he was to fortify his mind solely for his own advantage. This individualist theory must somehow be modified. The aim of the process I have described is not simply to indicate to the boy the amount of selfish pleasure which he can obtain from literary masterpieces; it is rather to show the boy that he is not alone and isolated, in a world where it is advisable for him to take and keep all that he can; but that he is one of a great fellowship of emotions and interests, and that his happiness depends upon his becoming aware of this, while his usefulness and nobleness must depend upon his disinterestedness, and upon the extent to which he is willing to share his advantages. The teaching of civics, as it is called, may be of some use in this direction, as showing a boy his points of contact with society. But no instruction in the constitution of society is profitable, unless somehow or other the dutiful motive is kindled, and the heroic virtue of service made beautiful.

When then I speak of the training of the imagination, I really mean the kindling of motive; and here again I claim that this must be based on a boy's own experience. He understands well enough the possibility of feeling emotion in relation to a small circle, his home and his immediate friends. But he is probably, like most young creatures, and indeed like a good many elderly ones, inclined to be suspicious of all that is strange and foreign, and to anticipate hostility or indifference. What he would willingly share with a relation or friend, he eagerly withholds from an outsider. To cultivate his imaginative sympathy, to give him an insight into the ways and thoughts of other men, to show to him that the same qualities which evoke his trust and love are not the monopoly of his own small circle—this is just what must be taught, because it is exactly what is not instinctively evolved.

The training of the imagination then is a deliberate effort to persuade the young to believe in the real nobility and beauty of life, in the great ideas which are moulding society and welding communities together. It cannot be done in a year or a decade; but it ought to be the first aim of education to initiate the imagination of the young into the idea of fellowship, and to make the thought of selfish individualism intolerable. It is not perhaps the only end of education, but I can hardly believe that it has any nobler or more sacred end.

IV

RELIGION AT SCHOOL

By W. W. VAUGHAN

The Master of Wellington College

"After all, how seldom does a Christian education teach one anything worth knowing about Christianity." These are the words of a man whom the public schools are proud to claim, a man who has seen Christian education, whether given in the elementary or in the secondary schools tested by the slow fires of peace, and by the quick devouring furnace of war. They seem at first sight to be a verdict of "guilty" against the teachers or the system in which they play a part. That verdict will not be accepted without protest by those incriminated, but even the protesters will feel some compunction, and now that they can no longer question the heroic "student" as to what he means, and go to him for advice as to the remedies for this failure, they should search their hearts and their experience for the help he might have given, had he not laid down his arms and his life on the Somme last autumn.

For long the need of help has been felt. The teaching of religion may have been less talked and written about, and less organised by societies and

associations, than have been other subjects dealt with
at school, but the problem of how best to make it
a living force in youth and an enduring force throughout the whole of life is often wrestled with at conferences of schoolmasters which do not publish their
proceedings, and by little groups of men who feel the
need of one another's help. It is certainly always
present in the minds, if not in the hearts, of every
head master, boarding-house master and tutor in
England. These know well what the difficulties are;
these know that a short cut to any subject is often
a long way round: that a short cut to religion leads
too often either to a slough of doubt or else to a
pharisaical hilltop, from which there is no path to
the great mountains where the Holy Spirit really
dwells.

It is never well to insist too much on difficulties,
but a bare statement of those that surround this
subject is needed. There are the difficulties of course
common to every subject; the difficulty of attracting
the real teacher, keeping him as a teacher, improving
him as a teacher when he has been attracted. Even
those who start out on their career with a determination that the teaching of religion at all events
should have its full share of their time and thought,
find that as their teaching life goes on and fresh duties
crowd in to usurp more and more all their energies,
that the time they can spare, and the thought they
can give, either to the preparation of their divinity
lessons, or to the enriching and cultivation of their
own souls, shrink. Now and then they are cruelly

disappointed at the result of their efforts as some conspicuous failure seems to prove their teaching vain; they are often depressed by the apparent apathy of the leaders of the Church, by their manifest reluctance even to allow others to make the new bottles which can alone hold the new wine.

Schoolmasters belong to a devoted and to a comparatively learned profession. They should belong, especially those who feel the needs—and all must to some extent—of the religious life of the school, also to a learning profession; and their learning should go beyond the experience of boyish failings, and boyish tragedies, and boyish virtues with which they are almost daily brought into contact; beyond the dictionaries and handbooks that enable the Bible lesson to be well prepared; it should go out into the books that deal with the philosophy and the history of religion—the books of Harnack and Illingworth, Hort and Inge, Bevan and Glover, and of others who make us feel how narrow our outlook on our religion is. It would of course be foolish to drag our pupils with us exactly to the point to which these books may have brought us after many years' experience, but it is essential that we should know of the existence of such a distant point if we are to give to those we teach any idea of there being beyond the limits that they can reach at school a great and wonderful and inspiring region which they, with the help of such leaders as have been mentioned can, nay must, explore for themselves if religion is to be something more than mere emotion, fitful in its working, liable to succumb to all the stronger emotions with which life attacks the citadel of the soul.

Another difficulty is that the teacher of religion is being more continuously and searchingly tested than the teacher of any other subject. The man who expatiates in the form-room on the beauties of literature, and is suspected of never reading a book is looked upon as merely a harmless fraud by those he teaches. The man who preaches, whether officially in the pulpit or unofficially in the class-room or study, a high standard of conduct, and is unsuccessful in his own efforts to attain it, depreciates for all the value of religion. Patience and industry and long-suffering and charitableness are virtues that bear the hall mark of Christianity, but they are virtues in which the best men fail continually, are conscious of their own failure and would plead for merciful judgment. If the parish priest is exposed to the criticism of those among whom he lives, a still fiercer light beats upon the pulpit or the desk of the schoolmaster. His consciousness of this sometimes leads him to reduce his teaching to the limits of his practice, instead of extending the former and having faith in his power to bring the latter up to this level. Indeed, when teachers and those who are taught are living so close together, both, from a not unworthy fear of insincerity, are liable to make themselves and their ideals out to be worse than they are. It is sympathy alone that can overcome this difficulty. Indeed, it is safe to say that without sympathy—sympathy that understands difficulties, working equally

in those who are old and those who are young—religion
at school must be a very cautious and probably a very
barren power.

Again, the schoolmaster is tempted, and even when
he is not tempted the boys credit him with yielding
to the temptation to treat religion as a super-police-
man: something to make discipline easy and consequently to make his own life smooth. It is no good
explaining too often that the aim is to get at religion
through discipline, but this aim should ever be before
us. Man cannot too early in life realise that discipline
of itself is valueless. Its inestimable value in war, as
in all the activities of life, is due to its being the necessary preliminary preparation for courageous action,
noble thought, wise self-control and unselfish self-sur-
render. But above all these difficulties, dominating
them all, affecting them all, perhaps poisoning them
all, is the fact, not to be escaped though it is often
ignored, that so many of the traditions of school life,
as of national life, seem founded on a basis opposed to
Christ's teaching. It is very hard to go through a day
of our lives, or even a short railway journey, and not
offend against the spirit of the Sermon on the Mount.
Older people have never been able to solve this
dilemma: the rulers find it more difficult than the ruled.
The whole of school life is stimulated by the principle
of competition, and kept together by a healthy and, on
the whole, a kindly self-assertion which is hard to
reconcile with the ideals that are upheld in the New
Testament. Yet at school, quite as much as in the
world, competition and self-assertion are tempered by

abundant friendliness and generosity; and at school, if not in the world, there are an increasing number of individuals who have so much spiritual power that they never need to exercise the more worldly power that clashes with the Beatitudes. Of this power boys seldom talk, except to some specially sympathetic ear at some specially heart-opening moment, but many are dumbly aware of it and they cultivate it, often unconsciously but to the great gain of those around them, by prayer and faithful worship. But even these richer natures are uncomfortably conscious that there is a conflict between what Christ commands and what the world advises. That conflict will not cease until faith has more power over our lives. It cannot grow naturally at school among boys, when it does not live in the nation among men; but it would indeed be faithless to miss, through fear of the world's withering power, any opportunity of quickening pure religion among the young. Though these opportunities vary very much in the day and the boarding school, they may be said to occur:

(1)   In the scripture lesson;

(2)   In the services whether held in chapel or, as is often the case especially in day schools, in the hall;

(3)   In the preparation for confirmation;

(4)   In all lessons in and out of school.

There is a great difference of opinion as to what should be taught in the scripture lesson, and who should teach it. It is easy enough to quote instances of extraordinary ignorance, to argue that, because a man who is in the trenches shocks his chaplain by his real or affected neglect of the facts of Bible history or the dogmas of the Church, therefore he has never had an opportunity of learning them; that same man would probably not give a much more impressive account of the profane subjects in the school curriculum. There is, too, the fact that a man may have forgotten everything of a subject and yet may have learnt much from it. Every teacher knows this, if every schoolboy does not. No one shrinks so much from revealing what he knows as the boy who is conscious that he has learnt a thing and is not sure that he can show his knowledge accurately. No subject has been left so free from what is supposed to be the sterilising influence of examinations as divinity. In many schools there have been one or two inspiring teachers of this subject who justify this system, but on the whole the result does not confirm the opinion that all would be well if we could have complete freedom from examinations. If in the future the harvest in religion is to be more worthy of the seed that is sown and the trouble of cultivation, we must face with more frankness, especially in the later years of a boy's life, all the difficulties that are presented by the problems of the Bible and Church History. We must have more courage in going beyond the syllabuses that are drawn up by universities and ecclesiastical societies. Both have to play for safety, but they are dull cards that this stake requires.

Teachers have overcome their timidity in dealing with the difficulties presented by the Old Testament. Very few now hesitate to take the book of Genesis, and, at all events if they are dealing with a high form, they let the boys see that the conflict between science and religion is only apparent, and that the victory of science does not mean the defeat of religion. If they have been lucky enough to use Driver's book on Genesis they will have felt on sure ground and any learner who has half understood it will have a shield against some of the weapons that assailed and defeated his father's generation. No teacher now would be afraid of making clear the problems presented by the book of Daniel or the book of Job, but when the New Testament is approached much more diffidence is felt, and indeed ought to be felt. Diffidence ought not however to involve silence.

A wise teacher has said that it is not the miracles of Christ but his standard that keeps men away from his Church, and therefore outside the influence for which the Church stands. True though this may be of men as life goes on, of the young it is not the whole truth. In those critical years of a man's religion—between eighteen and twenty-five—it is the sudden or the slow-growing doubt about the miracles of the New Testament, as much as the lofty standard that the "Follow me" of Christ requires, that makes the profession and even the holding of a religious faith so hard. More and more are the schools trying to prepare those in their charge for the perils that threaten the physical health and the character of the young; but it is tragic that they should be so unwilling to face frankly the perils that will sap the man's faith, and so expose his soul to the assaults of the world and the devil. It is very hard to put oneself in another's place; perhaps harder for the schoolmaster than for any other man, but when we are teaching such a subject as religion—a subject whose roots must perish if they cannot draw moisture from the springs of sincerity, we should try to imagine what must be the feelings of the thoughtful boy when he first discovers that the lessons which he has so often learnt and the Creeds that he has so often repeated were taken by his teachers in a sense which they carefully concealed from him. More harm is done by the economy of truth than by the suggestion of doubt.

It may be extraordinarily difficult to treat these problems of the New Testament with becoming reverence; but is it not true to say that the day when it becomes easy to any man to do so will be the day when he ought to stop dealing with them? The real irreverence, the only irreverence, is the glib confidence of the ignorant or the cynical concealment of one who knows but dare not tell. What idea of the New Testament does the average boy who leaves, say in the fifth form, carry away with him from his public school? He may know that certain facts are told in one Gospel and not in another; that there are certain inconsistencies in the accounts given by the different Synoptic Gospels of the same miracle, or what is apparently the same miracle. He may be able to explain the parables more fully than their author ever meant them to be explained; he may have at his fingers' ends St Paul's journeys and even have been thrilled by St Paul's shipwreck, but he will probably have missed the meaning of the good news for himself and the power to treasure it for his life's strength.

This failure to appreciate and to accept the challenge of religion—a failure shown later on in life in a certain diffidence about foreign missions, and in the toleration of social conditions that deny Christ as flatly as ever Peter did—is not the fault of the schools alone. The schools only reflect the world outside and the homes from which they are recruited. In neither is there as much light as there should be. The difficulty of the vicious circle dominates this as so many other problems. School reacts on the world, the world on the home[1] and the home on school, the blame cannot be apportioned, need not be apportioned; how the circle can be broken it is much more important to determine. From time to time it has been broken, so decisively too that for a while the riddle seems solved, at all events the old way is abandoned for ever. Arnold's work at Rugby must have involved such a breach. His work has never had to be done all over again and there have been many to keep it in repair, but it needs to be extended now in the light of new problems, scientific, social and international. For this, as for all other extensions, courage is needed. The courage to face the difficulties that modern research and modern thought involve and the courage to point out that our Lord, though in his short career he changed the bias of men's lives, never claimed to leave man a detailed

---

[1] Nothing is said here about the co-operation of the home with the school. In religion as in all other matters it is assumed. The influence of the home cannot be exaggerated but schoolmasters must resist the temptation to shift the burden of responsibility for any failure on to other shoulders.

guide for conduct or for happiness. It was to a simple society that he taught the laws of purity and love, he did not extend the range of their application beyond the needs of the Pharisee, the Sadducee, the Scribe, the peasant and the dweller in the little towns through which he shed the light of his presence. These laws sanctify the whole of life because they dominate the heart, from which all life must spring, but they do not answer all questions about all the subordinate provinces of life. The arts in their narrow sense, philosophy, even pleasure, they pass by. Man will not neglect the one or distort the other if he has really breathed the spirit of Christ, but at times the urgency of his Master's business will seem to shut them out of his life.

All this needs learning by the old, and explaining to the young, for otherwise life will be one-sided, and when the day comes, as come it must to those who think, when a choice must be made, and there seems no alternative to following literally in Christ's footsteps and turning the back on much of the beauty and the thrill of the world, bewilderment will seize the chooser and at the best he will dedicate himself to a joyless and unattractive puritanism, or surrender himself to a rudderless voyage across the ocean of life. Religion at school must touch with its refining power the impulses, aesthetic and intellectual, that become powerful in late boyhood and early manhood. If, as so often is the case, it ignores their existence, or endeavours to starve them, they may well assert themselves with fatal power, to coarsen and degrade the whole of life.

The scripture lesson will indeed miss its opportunity if it does not, in the later stages of a boy's career, set him thinking on these subjects, and help him to a wise appreciation of the holiness of beauty, as well as of the beauty of holiness. To accomplish this task the language of the Bible itself gives noble help. All the qualities of great literature shine forth from it and it should put to shame and flight the tawdry and the melodramatic. It is an ill service not to make all familiar with the actual words of Holy Writ. Commentaries and Bible histories may be at times convenient tools, but they are only tools, and accurate knowledge of what they teach is no compensation for a want of respectful familiarity with the text itself.

Hardly less important for good and evil are the chapel services. They are much attacked. It has been argued that public worship is distasteful in later life because of the compulsory chapels of boyhood. If this were really so, evidence should be forthcoming that those who come from schools where there is no compulsory attendance at chapel, because there is no chapel to attend, are more eager to avail themselves of the opportunities offered by college chapels than are their more chapel ridden contemporaries. No one, however, can be quite satisfied that chapel services are as helpful as they might be. The difficulty is how to improve them. The suggestion that they should all be voluntary is at first sight attractive but there are two insuperable difficulties. The one is the power of fashion, for it might well become fashionable in a certain house not to attend chapel. Those who know anything of the inside of schools know how such a fashion would deter many of the best boys from going, and martyrdom ought not to be part of the training of school life. The other difficulty is more subtle, but none the less real, it originates in the boys' quite healthy fear of claiming merit. Those in authority, if wise, would not count attendance at chapel for righteousness, but some of the most sensitive boys might think that they would do so, and might stay away in consequence, and thus deprive themselves of something they really valued. Two or three, not many, might come from a wrong motive, and perhaps these would stay to pray, but they would be no compensation for the loss of the others.

From time to time it is possible to have voluntary services, and attendance at Holy Communion should always be voluntary, not only in name but in fact. On the whole it is better that a boy who neglects this duty should go on neglecting it, than that those who come should feel that their presence is noted with approval or the reverse.

But it is different with the daily service. Irksome it may sometimes be, not only to boys; but half its virtue lies in the fact that all are there in body and may sometimes be there in spirit too. The familiarity of the oft-repeated prayers and the oft-sung hymns leads to inattention perhaps, but seldom, it may be hoped, to callousness; religious emotion may only occasionally be stirred but the thread of natural piety, binding man to man and man to God, is strengthened, as fresh strands are added. At the least it may be

claimed for the chapel services that they rescue from
our hours of business some minutes each day in which
our thoughts are free to make their way to the throne
of God.   Christ's promise to bring rest to those who
come to him has been fulfilled in many a school chapel.
Those of us who have had to pass through the valley
of sorrow and temptation and loneliness—and who
has not?—know that this is no mean claim.   Boys,
even men, often grumble at what they really value.
To do so is our national defect, misleading to the
onlooker.   The truth is, we are so fearful of being
accused of casting our pearls before swine, that we
often pretend, even to ourselves, that what we know
to be the most precious pearl in our possession is
valueless.

Most masters and boys would agree that, in the
few weeks preceding confirmation, the religious life is
deepest and most sincere.   There is a moving of the
waters then, and many make the effort, and step in,
and are made whole for the time at all events.   As to
what exactly goes on in the mind of anyone at such
a time there can be no certainty.   There is the obvious
danger of a reaction, and, guard against it as one may,
it exists and sometimes leads to disaster; but there is
another danger to which the schoolmaster is then
liable, it is the danger of making confirmation an
occasion for much talk on sexual difficulties.   The
existence of these should be faced, but at any time
rather than at confirmation, except so far as they occur
quite naturally in dealing with the commandments.

It is a real disaster for a child to associate this time,

when he should be trying to shoulder enthusiastically his responsibilities as a citizen of God's Kingdom upon earth, with any particular sin. He must indeed overcome evil, but he must overcome it with good. It is on good that his eyes should be fixed. It is towards the Lord of all that is good that his heart should be uplifted. Anyone who has had to do with this time knows what it means in a boy's religious life, how reluctant he is to speak of it, how perilous it is to disturb his reluctance by inquisitive question or excessive exhortation. He knows, too, how much his own nature has gained by contact at such times with the reverent stirrings of less world-stained souls, how wondrous has been the spiritual refreshment that has come to him from the unconscious witness of the younger heart.

For most boys it is a loss not to be confirmed at school, which for the time is the centre of their energies, their hopes, their disappointments and their temptations; but the loss to the masters who share their preparation would be irreparable. They may sometimes blunder from want of knowledge and experience, but their will to help is strong, and perhaps not least persuasive when chastened by diffidence.

But all these scripture lessons, chapel services and confirmation preparation will be powerless to produce a Christian education, if they be not held together by every lesson and by the whole life of the school. Industry and obedience, truthfulness and fidelity to duty, unselfishness and thoroughness, must form the soil without which no religious plant can grow; and

these are taught and learnt in the struggle with Latin
prose, or mathematics, or French grammar, or scientific formula; as well as in the cricket field, on the
football ground, in the give and take, the pains and
the pleasures of daily life.

It is hard for us in England to imagine a purely
secular education, the very buildings of many of our
schools would protest against it; perhaps it is equally
difficult for us to realise how far we fall short of what
we might accomplish did the spirit of Christianity
really inform our lives.

To-day is our opportunity. The claims of education are being listened to as they never have been in
England. Money in millions is being promised, the
value of this subject or that is being canvassed, the
most venerable traditions are being shaken. It is a
time of hope, but a time of danger too. All sorts of
plans are being formed for breaking down the partition
walls that divide man from man, and class from class,
and nation from nation; there is only one plan that
will not leave the ground encumbered by ruins.

That is the plan of which good men in all ages have
caught glimpses, and which the Son of Man set out for
us to follow. The peril now lies, not in the fact of
nothing being done, but in some starved idea of a
narrow patriotism.

The war has surely taught two lessons;—one that
the efforts we made before 1914 to guard our country
from spiritual and moral foes were shamefully trivial
compared with those we have made since to keep our
visible foe at bay; the other that our responsibilities

for the future, if we are to justify our claims to be the champions of justice and weakness, can never be borne unless we learn ourselves, and teach each generation as it grows up, to face the fierce light that shines from heaven. All sorts of devices, ecclesiastical and political have been adopted to break up that light and make it tolerable for our weak eyes. Men have been so afraid of children being blinded by it that they have allowed them to sit, some in darkness, and others in the twilight of compromise.

It has been said that for the average man in the ancient world there existed two main guides and sanctions for his conduct of life, namely the welfare of his city, and the laws and traditions of his ancestors. Has the average man much wiser guides or stronger sanctions now? Is a much nobler appeal made to the children of England than was made to the children of Athens? Just before Joshua led his people over the Jordan, he instructed them how the ark of the covenant was to go before them and a space to be left between them and it, so that they might know the way by which they must go, *for they had not passed this way before.* Once again a river of decision has to be crossed, a road has to be trodden along which men have not passed before. Whether we speak of reconstruction or a new start or use any other metaphor to show our conviction that war has changed all things, the idea is the same. We must see to it that the ark of the covenant is borne before our nation and our schools, along the way that is new and still full of stones of stumbling.

Either the old landmarks have disappeared or a new land has to be explored. Somehow, all things have to be made new, for even the spiritual things have been destroyed or are found wanting. It is to the schools, to the homes, to the mothers of England that the richest opportunity comes. If they can solve the difficulty of making the Christian education and the Christian life react upon one another the partition walls between religion and conduct will be broken down for every age. Intentionally or unintentionally, these walls have been built up, perhaps by the teachers and parents, certainly by the conventions of life. The result is that though there is more true religion in the schools than is acknowledged by those outside and than those within care to boast of, and though the standard of conduct is not ignoble, there is too little fusion; both components are brittle, they cannot stand the strain of sudden temptation, they lack enduring power. No one will forget how in those first months of war, consolation was offered even from pulpits for all the horrors and the sadness and the waste of conflict in the thought that as a nation we should be purged of selfishness, of luxury, of sensuality, of all the vices that peace engenders. That is surely a shameful confession, that our religion had been in vain. We had to wait for, and partake in, a three years' orgy of cruelty and violence to learn what our Lord had taught us in three years of gentleness. If we are going to teach the same lessons about war when peace is made, to keep alive the fires of hate, and to keep smouldering the embers of suspicion, we shall be confessing that a Christian education cannot teach us anything about Christianity.

The student in arms would not have had us despair. Peace when it comes will make demands on our fortitude. There will be many lying in the no-man's land between vice and virtue who will need to be rescued at great risk. There will be many forlorn hopes to be led against disease, the foster child of vice, that has gained strength under the cover of war. The disappointing days of peace will give an opportunity for the development of Christian qualities fully as great as the bracing days of battle. Teachers will need to gird up their loins for the task of giving a wise welcome to the thousands that an awakened State will send to sit at their feet, and unless they can give spiritual food as well as worldly wisdom and paying knowledge, the souls of the new-comers will be starved beyond the remedy of any free meals. How to spiritualise education is the real problem, for it is only by a spiritualised education that we can escape from the avalanche of materialism that is hanging over the European world just now. No syllabus, no act of Parliament can do this. There is no royal road which all can travel. It has been done, to some extent, in the past, and it will have to be done, to a much greater extent, in the future by the layman and the laywoman, by the teachers of all denominations, by some even whom inspectors may consider inefficient and whom children may tolerate as queer. It will be done best by the best teachers, but all teachers can share in the work on the one condition that they have consciously or unconsciously dedicated themselves to the task. For a teacher to write much about it is impossible, he must know how greatly he has failed. And he has not the recompense that comes to many who fail, in the shape of certain knowledge why success has been withheld.

That his failure is shared by those who strive to make religion move the world of men is no consolation. Indeed, that thought might make him hopeless did it not suggest that the aims and methods of both may be wrong. It is possible to have hoped too much from the school chapels being full, it is possible to fear too much from the churches being empty. Piety is no doubt fostered by attendance at a religious service, but there is some distance between piety and true religion. It would probably not be untrue to say that Christian education has seemed more concerned with the ceremonial duties of religion than with its spiritual enthusiasm, more eager about faith in some particular explanation of the past than about faith in a re-creation of the future, more attentive to the machinery of the organisation of the Church than to the words and commands of its Founder. As the Church has become more powerful in the world, it has lost its power over men's hearts. To some it has seemed an institution for the relief of poverty, to others the support of the "haves" against the "have-nots," but to too few has it been the home of spiritual adventures, the maintainer of spiritual values. Men have escaped from the relentless simplicity of the Master's commands by attention to the complicated

machinery which disregard of them has made necessary. This may not have been consciously marked
by the young, but the atmosphere of religion that they
have had to breathe has been the tired atmosphere of
the ecclesiastical workshop, and not the bracing air of
free service. Some restoration of the hopefulness of
the early Christians is needed; hopefulness is not now
the note of what is taught, though with it is sometimes confused the boisterous cheerfulness that is
wrongly supposed to attract the young. The appeal
of the Church must be based on looking forward, not
backward, on hope, rather than on repentance.

The Church will have less to do with the world
than it had in the past, because it will have shaken off
the fetters of the world: it will not be always explaining
to the young how they can enjoy the world and yet
deny the world: it will not need to explain itself so
often, to insist so pathetically on the superiority of
its own channels of influence, but it will attract to
itself, or rather to the work that it is trying to do—
for it will have forgotten self—all the adventurous
spirits who are prepared to risk pain and failure as
fellow-workers in fulfilling the purposes of God in the
world. What is worth knowing about Christianity is
surely first and foremost that it is a leaven that might
leaven the whole world; and that until that leaven
works in each individual heart, in each society, where
two or three are gathered together, Christ's presence
cannot be claimed. As this knowledge is gained, it
will be possible for the learner to know in his heart,
and not merely by heart, what is meant by the great

mysterious terms Incarnation, Atonement, Resurrection; as this knowledge is tested and proved true by experience of life, the meaning and power of prayer will become clearer. A clue will have been put into the hand of each as he travels along the way which he has not passed heretofore. It will not lead all by the same path but it will lead all towards that "great and high mountain," whence "that great city, the Holy Jerusalem" may be seen. If the teacher is wise, when the mountain top is nigh and before that vision breaks upon his fellow-traveller's sight, he will stand aside with thankful heart, and close his task with the prayer that the Glory of God may shine more brightly and more continuously on the newcomer, than it has shone on him.

V

CITIZENSHIP

By A. MANSBRIDGE
Founder of the Workers' Educational Association

I

DIRECT TRAINING FOR CITIZENSHIP

There is no institution in national life which can free itself from the responsibility of training for citizenship those who come under its influence, whether they be men or women. The problem is common to all institutions, although it may present itself in diverse forms appropriate to varying ages and experiences. It is primarily the problem of all schools and places of education.

The aim of education, according to Comenius, is "to train generally all who are born to all that is human." From that definition it follows that the purpose of any school must be to bear its part in developing to the utmost the powers of body, mind and spirit for the common good. It must be to secure the application of the finest attributes of the race to the work of developing citizenship, which is the art of living together on the highest plane of human life.

Citizenship is, in reality, the focusing point of all human virtues though it is often illuminated by the consciousness of a city not made with hands. It represents in a practical form the spirit of courage, unselfishness and sympathy consecrated to service in time of war and peace. Generally speaking, in England and her Dominions, citizenship is developed in harmony with an ideal of democracy.

"The progress of democracy is irresistible," says De Tocqueville, "because it is the most uniform, the most ancient and the most permanent tendency to be found in history."

But its right working is dependent entirely upon uplift not only of mind but of spirit. The democratic community, above all other communities, must have within itself schools which at one and the same time impart information concerning the theory and methods of its government and inspire consecration to social service rather than to individual welfare, schools which reveal the transcendence of the interests of the State as compared with the interests of any individual or group of individuals within it. The democratic State has been compared to "one huge Christian personality, one mighty growth or stature of an honest man." Out of this comparison arises the idea of citizenship reaching out beyond the boundaries of a single State —one honest man among many—and thus responsibility is placed upon the schools to develop knowledge of, and sympathy with, the activities and aspirations of human life in many nations. The comity of nations depends directly upon the intellectual and spiritual honesty which obtains in each of them, and true strength of nationality arises more from the exercise of these qualities than from extent of area or of productive power.

Every subject taught in a school should serve the needs of the larger citizenship; if it fails to do so it is either wrongly taught or superfluous.

Social welfare depends upon the right use of knowledge by the individual, however restricted or developed that knowledge may be, whether it be acquired in elementary school or university.

There has been much discussion concerning the relative importance of the development of community spirit in the schools and the introduction of the direct teaching of citizenship. The methods are not mutually exclusive; their operations are distinct. The school which does not develop community spirit, which does not fit into its place in the work of training the complete man, is obviously imperfect. The same cannot be said of the school which does not provide direct instruction in citizenship; for teaching may be given in so many indirect ways. Some consideration of what has happened in this connection both in England and America will perhaps be most helpful, although the intangible nature of the results would render dangerous any attempt to make definite pronouncements on their success or failure.

Largely as the result of the realisation of the immediate relationship between national education and national productivity there are abundant signs that the English educational system is about to be

developed. The ordinary argument has been well
put:

> A new national spirit has been aroused in our people by the war;
> if we are to recover and improve our position at the end of the war
> that national spirit must be maintained; for unless every man and
> woman comes to know and feel that industry, agriculture, commerce,
> shipping, and credit, are national concerns, and that education is a
> potent means for the promotion of these objects among others, we
> shall fail in the great effort of national recuperation. In plainer
> words, our great firms will not make money, wages will fall, and
> wage-earners will be out of work[1].

The possibility of the extension of the educational
system to meet the needs of technical training need
not cause disquiet among those whose desire is for
fulness of citizenship, if they are prepared to insist
that teachers shall be trained on broad and comprehensive lines and that every vocational course shall
include instruction in direct citizenship. The argument
is ready to hand and simple. If all men and women
must strive to work wisely and well, so also should they
learn how to participate in the government, local and
national, which their work supports. Moreover the
right study of a trade or profession induces a percep-
tion of the inter-relationship of all human activity.

On the other hand it is important that vocational
work, at least so far as it is carried out by manual
training, should be introduced into schemes of liberal
education. In this connection it is worth recalling
that in a recent report, the Consultative Committee
of the Board of Education expressed with complete

---

[1] *Interim Report of the Consultative Committee of the Board of Education
on Scholarships for Higher Education, May,* 1916.

conviction the opinion that manual training was indispensable in places of secondary education:

> We consider that our secondary education has been too exclusively concerned with the cultivation of the mind by means of books and the instruction of the teacher. To this essential aim there must be added as a condition of balance and completeness that of fostering those qualities of mind and that skill of hand which are evoked by systematic work.

In this way would be generated that "sympathetic and understanding contact between all brainworkers and the complete men who work with both hands and brain" so strongly pleaded for by Professor Lethaby who insists that "some teaching about the service of labour must be got into all our educational schemes."

It must be remembered that the question of vocational training affects chiefly the proposed system of compulsory continuation school education up to the age of eighteen, which has yet to be established for all boys and girls not in attendance at secondary schools or who have not completed a satisfactory period of attendance[1].

The inadequacy of the period of education allotted to the vast mass of the population and the need for educational reform in many directions can only be noted; both these matters however affect citizenship profoundly.

It is upon the expectation of early development on the following lines, indicated without detail, that our

[1] See *Final Report of the Departmental Committee on Juvenile Education in Relation to Employment after the War*, 1917, Cd. 8512. The Bill "to make further provision with respect to Education in England and Wales and for purposes connected therewith" [Bill 89], had not been introduced by Mr Fisher when this article was written.

consideration of the possibilities of schools in regard to citizenship must be based:

(1) A longer period of elementary school life during which no child shall be employed for other than educational purposes.

(2) The establishment of compulsory continuation schools for all boys and girls up to the age of eighteen, the hours of attendance to be allowed out of reasonable working hours.

(3) Complete opportunity for qualified boys and girls to continue their technical or humane studies from the elementary school to the university.

(4) A distinct improvement in the supply and power of teachers, chiefly as the result of better training in connection with universities and the establishment of a remuneration which will enable them to live in the manner demanded by the nature and responsibilities of their calling.

The two main aspects of the development of citizenship through the schools which have already been noted may be summarised as follows, and may be considered separately:

(1) The direct teaching of civics or of citizenship;

(2) The development through the ordinary school community of the qualities of the good citizen.

THE DIRECT STUDY OF CITIZENSHIP

The study in schools of civic relations has been developed to a much greater extent in America than in England. This is probably due largely to the fact that the American need is the more obvious. In normal times, there is a constant influx of people of different nationalities to the United States whom it is the aim of the government to make into American citizens. At the same time there is in America a greater disposition than in England to adapt abstract study to practical ends, to link the class-room to the factory, to the city hall, and to the Capitol itself. As one of her scholars says:

> Both the inspiration and the romance of the scholar's life lie in the perfect assurance that any truth, however remote or isolated, has its part in the unity of the world of truth and its undreamed of applicability to service[1].

There are in America numerous societies, among them the National Education Association, the American Historical Association, the National Municipal League, the American Political Science Association, which are working steadily to make the study of civics an essential feature of every part of the educational system. Their prime purposes are summarised as follows:

> (1) To awaken a knowledge of the fact that the citizen is in a social environment whose laws bind him for his own good;
> (2) To acquaint the citizen with the forms of organisation and methods of administration of government in its several departments[2].

They claim that this can best be done by means of bringing the young citizen into direct contact with the significant facts of the life of his own local community and of the national community. To indicate

[1] Peabody, *The Religion of an Educated Man.*
[2] Haines, *The Teaching of Government.*

this more clearly they have applied to the study the name of "Community Civics."

The argument that a sense of unreality may arise as a result of the apparent completeness of knowledge gained in the school is met by the close contact maintained all the time with the community outside.

There is unanimity of opinion that civics shall be taught from the elementary school onwards:

"We believe," runs the report of the Committee of Eight of the American Historical Association, "that elementary civics should permeate the entire school life of the child. In the early grades the most effective features of this instruction will be directly connected with the teaching of regular subjects in the course of study. Through story, poem and song there is the quickening of those emotions which influence civic life. The works and biographies of great men furnish many opportunities for incidental instruction in civics. The elements of geography serve to emphasise the interdependence of men—the very earliest lesson in civic instruction. A study of pictures and architecture arouses the desire for civic beauty and orderliness[1]."

A recent inquiry by a Committee of the American Political Science Association makes it quite clear that the subject is actually taught in the bulk of the elementary and secondary schools of the various States and that generally the results are satisfactory, or indicate clearly necessary reforms. The difficulty of providing suitable text-books is partly met by the addition of supplementary local information.

There are very few colleges and universities which do not provide courses in political science.

No claim is made that the teaching of civics makes of necessity good citizens, but merely that it makes

[1] Haines, *The Teaching of Government.*

the good citizen into a better one. The justification of the subject lies in its own content.

It is a study of an important phase of human society and, for this reason, has the same value as elementary science or history[1].

There is, moreover, throughout the various American reports, an insistence on the power of the community ideal in the school and the necessity for discipline in the performance of school duties and a due appreciation of the importance of individual action in relation to the class and to the school.

In England there has been much general and unco ordinated advocacy of the direct teaching of citizenship, but, for various reasons, it does not appear to have been introduced generally into the schools, nor does there appear to be any immediate likelihood of development in the existing schools.

The Civic and Moral Education League made definite inquiry, in 1915, of teachers and schools. They pronounced the results to be disappointing, though they comforted themselves with the incontrovertible dictum that "the people who are doing most have least time to talk about it." As the result of their inquiry, they drew up a statement of the aims of civics which in general and in detail differed little from the ideas accepted in America.

If compulsory continued education is introduced, for boys and girls who now have no school education after the elementary school, it is of the utmost importance that the direct study should be included in

[1] Bourne, *The Teaching of History and Civics in the Elementary and the Secondary School.*

some form or other before the age of eighteen is reached, and it is in connection with this type of school rather than in connection with the elementary or secondary school that constructive efforts should be made.

It must be remembered that Mr Acland, when Minister for Education, introduced the subject into the Elementary Code of 1895 and provided a detailed syllabus. This was generally approved not only as the action of a progressive administrator but as an evidence of the new spirit of freedom beginning to reveal itself in the educational system.

There are some education authorities, like the County of Chester, which enact that the study of citizenship shall proceed side by side with religious education, but the majority leave it to the teachers to do all that is necessary by the adaptation of other subjects and the development of school spirit.

The elaborate nature of Mr Acland's syllabus tended to defeat its object, and some held it to be psychologically unsound, but there has also been lack of suitable text-books. In general, however, the whole subject depends peculiarly upon the personality of the teacher who feels no lack of text-books if he is alive to the interest of his lesson.

In *Studies in Board Schools*[1], there is a delightful study of a lesson on "Rates" to young citizens with the altruistic text, "All for Each, Each for All." "Citizen Carrots," a tired newspaper boy up every morning at five, is revealed as responding with great enthusiasm to this interesting lesson which

[1] Charles Morley, 1897.

commences with a drawing on a blackboard of a "regulation workhouse, a board school, a free library, a lamp post, a water-cart, a dustman, a policeman, a steam roller, a navvy or two, and a long-handled shovel stuck in a heap of soil." A hypothetical payer of rates, "Mrs Smith," is revealed as getting a great deal for her rates:

She is protected from any harm; her property is safe; she can walk about the streets with comfort by day or night; her drains are seen to; her rubbish is taken away for her; she has books and newspapers to read; if she has ten children, she can have them well taught for nothing—so that if they are willing to learn, and attend school regularly, they can very easily make their own living when they grow up; if she is ill, she can go to the infirmary for medicine; and if, when she grows old, she is unable to pay rent or buy food or clothes, these things are provided for her.

"And please, sir, the Parks," interjected the eager Carrots.

If the definition of a good citizen propounded by Professor Masterman is true—that he is one who pays his rates without grumbling—"Citizen Carrots," whatever his disadvantages, is intellectually anyhow on the way to become such a citizen, and certainly in the sketch, "Citizen Carrots" is determined that the rates shall be expended properly because he himself will have a vote in later days.

It is probable that lessons such as these are more frequent than the time-tables would indicate. There are few head masters of elementary schools who would disclaim the adequate teaching of citizenship in their schools. They would explain that the treatment of history and geography proceeding from local standpoints was effective in this direction, and it is the rule rather than otherwise for visits to be paid to places of historic interest within reach of the schools. Advantage is also taken of such days as Empire Day to stimulate interest in the State, as well as to impart knowledge concerning its organisation. All this is reinforced by the use of appropriate reading books which are instruments of indirect, but not necessarily less effective, instruction.

The larger opportunities which secondary schools offer have not been taken advantage of to induce the specific study of civics to any greater extent than in the elementary schools, although many schools are able to devote at least a period each week to the consideration of current events, and, naturally, the teaching of history and geography includes much more completely the consideration of institutions both at home and abroad.

The idea of the regional or local survey is gaining ground and in some respects it will prove to serve the same purpose as the "Community Civics" of the American high school.

There have been attempts to introduce economics into the secondary school curriculum, but they have not persisted to any extent. In the *Memorandum on Curricula of Secondary Schools* issued by the Board of Education in 1913, it is suggested that "it will sometimes be desirable to provide, for those who propose on leaving school to enter business, a special commercial course with special study of the more technical side of economic theory and some study of political and constitutional history." For the rest there is no mention of the subjects intimately connected with government. It is clear that the Board expects that out of the subjects of the ordinary curriculum, with such special efforts suggested by public interest as may from time to time occur, the student will gain a general knowledge of the affairs of the community round about, some knowledge of the principles of politics, clear ideas concerning movements for social reform, and some acquaintance with international problems. If he does so, he will have secured a useful introduction to the studies associated with adult life.

An intelligent study of languages will help materially in this direction and, whilst this is specially true in the cases of Greek and Latin, there is no reason why modern languages should not serve the same purpose. It is, however, often the case that the study of the history and institutions of modern countries is not associated sufficiently with the study of their language.

The public and grammar schools of England, as contrasted with the newer secondary schools, are more especially the homes of classical studies, and it is through the working of these schools that the knowledge of institutions in ancient Greece and Rome will have its greatest effect on citizenship.

The study of political science as a specific subject is gaining ground in universities, whilst the study of the Empire and its institutions has naturally made rapid progress during the last few years. There may also be noted distinct tendencies, arising out of the experience of the war, towards the foundation of schools destined to deal with the institutions and the thought of foreign countries. In the schools of economics and history there is fulness of attempt to study all that can be included under the generic title of civics which, after all, may be defined as political and social science interpreted in immediate and practical ways.

II

INDIRECT TRAINING FOR CITIZENSHIP

After all is said and done the ideal training for citizenship in the schools depends more upon the wisdom engendered in the pupil than upon the direct study of civics. If the spirits of men and women are set in a right direction they will reach out for knowledge as for hid treasure. "Wisdom is more moving than any motion; she passeth and goeth through all things by reason of her pureness[1]."

It happens also in natural sequence that the spirit developed in a school will lead to the construction of institutions in connection with school life calculated to secure its adequate expression.

Elementary schools, however, are much handicapped in this way. If it comes about that work other than educational or recreative is forbidden to children during the years of attendance at school, and also that the period of school life is lengthened, there will be opportunity for the development of games on a self-governing basis. Elementary school

[1] *Wisdom of Solomon,* vii. 24.

children have a large measure of initiative; all they need is a real chance to exercise it. They would willingly make their schools real centres of child life. Many children at present have little else than narrow tenements and the streets, out of which influences arise which war continually against the social influences of the school.

The opportunity afforded by well-ordered leisure would be accentuated by the more complete operation of movements such as boys' brigades, boy scouts, girl guides, and Church lads' brigades, which are in their several ways doing much to develop citizenship. Such bodies are now in effect educational authorities, and classes are organised by them in connection with the Board of Education.

There have been many attempts to introduce self-governing experiments into elementary schools and, whilst they have often been defeated by reason of the immaturity of the children, yet some of them have met with great success. The election of monitors on the lines of a general election is an instance of success in this direction. The ideas which have arisen from the advocacy of the Montessori system have induced methods of greater freedom in connection with many aspects of elementary school life. The Caldecott Community, dealing with working-class children in the neighbourhood of St Pancras, has tried many interesting experiments. That, however, of the introduction of children's courts of justice had to be abandoned, but not until many valuable lessons in child psychology had been learnt.

Side by side with the elementary school, there are rising in England experiments similar to those undertaken by such organisations as the School City and the George Junior Republics of America. The most notable among them is the Little Commonwealth, Dorchester, which has achieved astonishing results through the process of taking delinquent children and allowing them self-government. But, hopeful as the prospects are, their ultimate effect will be best estimated when their pupils, restored in youth to the honourable service of the community, are taking their full share in life as adult citizens, and naturally every care is taken in the organisation of these institutions to ensure that the transition from their sheltered citizenship to the outside world shall not be of so abrupt a nature as to tend to render unreal and remote the life in which the children have taken part.

Nearly all of the more recent experiments in regard to the school and its kindred institutions are co-operative in principle and in method, but it is probably Utopian to conceive an educational method which shall achieve the highest success without having included within it the element of competition. If competition is a method obtaining outside the school it is bound to reproduce itself within it. The only possible thing for the school to do is to restrict the influence of competition to the channels where it can be beneficial.

The method by which elementary school children pass to the secondary school is by means of competitive scholarships. In common with the Consultative

Committee of the Board of Education it is necessary to accept the fact that at present "the scholarship system is too firmly rooted in the manner, habits and character of this country to be dislodged, even if it were thrice condemned by theory[1]." But, in the interests of citizenship, scholarships should be awarded as the result of non-competitive tests, if only to secure that every child shall receive the education for which he or she is fitted.

The stress and strain imposed upon many who climb the ladder of education, often occasioned by the inadequacy of the scholarship for the purposes to which it is to be applied, tend to develop characteristics which are so strongly individual as to be distinctly anti-social.

It is unfortunate that in many subjects of the curriculum it is not merely bad form to help one's neighbour but distinctly a school sin, and this makes it necessary for a balance to be struck by the introduction of subjects at which all can work for the good of the class or the school. Manual work and local surveys are subjects of this nature and should be encouraged side by side with games of which there are three essential aspects:—the individual achievement, the winning of the match or race, and "playing the game." In reference to citizenship the last of these is the only one which ultimately matters.

It is generally admitted that the great public schools are those which are most characteristic of

[1] *Interim Report of the Consultative Committee of the Board of Education on Scholarships for Higher Eaucation,* 1916.

English boy life at its best. Glorying as they do in a splendid tradition, they have always had in addition the opportunity of adapting themselves to new needs. Their reform is always under discussion and perchance they are waiting even now for some Arnold or Thring to lead them in a new England, for new it will inevitably be. Even so, the sense of responsibility they have developed has been translated into the terms of English government over half the world.

The objective of the public school boy anxious to take a part in government at home has always been parliament, or such local institutions as demand his service in accordance with the tradition of his family. The tendency to despise the homely duties of a city councillor or poor law guardian is, however, passing. There are few schools which do not welcome visitors to speak to the boys who have first-hand acquaintance with the life of the poor or who are indeed of that life themselves. In this way boys get to realise, as far as it is possible through sympathy, what it means to be out of work, what it means to be hungry for unattainable learning, what children have to suffer, and, in addition to the practical interest which many boys immediately develop, it cannot be doubted that many ideals for the conduct of social life in the future are conceived, even if dimly, for the first time. Thanks to the unremitting efforts of large-minded head masters, public school boys more and more realise that they are beneficiaries of the spirit of a past day, not only in the sense of the creation of a noble tradition but actually in regard to the material provision of buildings and the financial support of teaching.

There is likely to be an extension of university education in the near future. The ancient universities of Oxford and Cambridge with their great college system will be strengthened, as will be the universities which were established at the end of the nineteenth and the beginning of the twentieth centuries. The demand for the better training of teachers will result inevitably in the creation of more universities. The inadequate sum which this country has spent upon university education up to the present will be greatly increased.

As a direct result of the opportunity which university life gives to undergraduates for the development of self-governing institutions, there can be little doubt that the university must be regarded above all other schools and most institutions as powerful in the development of good citizenship. The public school tradition will be carried directly into the older universities and in increasing measure into the new universities as the best spirit of the public schools gradually permeates the whole system of our education even down to the elementary schools themselves. When these opportunities so lavishly provided for the development of student life in its self-governing aspects are realised and when above it all there stand great teachers in the lineage of those described by Cardinal Newman in his eulogy of Athens—"the very presence of Plato" to the student, "a stay for his mind to rest on, a burning thought in his heart, a bond of union with men like himself, ever afterwards "—little else can be desired. In every university there must be such teachers, or universities will tend to fall to the level of the life about them. "You can infuse," said Lord Rosebery at the Congress of the Universities of the Empire, "character, and morals and energy and patriotism by the tone and atmosphere of your university and your professors."

From one point of view, all the old universities of Europe—Bologna, Paris, Prague, Oxford, Cambridge, etc.—must be regarded as definite and conscious protests against the dividing and isolating—the anti-civic—forces of the periods of their institution. They represent historically the development of communities for common interest and protection in the great and holy cause of the pursuit of learning, and above all things their story is the story of the growth of European unity and citizenship.

The feudal and ecclesiastical order of the old mediaeval world were both alike threatened by the power that had so strangely sprung up in the midst of them. Feudalism rested on local isolation, on the severance of kingdom from kingdom and barony from barony, on the distinction of blood and race, on the supremacy of material or brute force, on an allegiance determined by accidents of place and social position. The University, on the other hand, was a protest against this isolation of man from man. The smallest school was European and not local[1].

The spirit which is characteristic of a university in its best aspects, linked with the spirit which is inherent in the ranks of working people, has on more

[1] J. R. Green, *A Short History of the English People*.

occasions than one set on foot movements for the education of the people. One of the most notable instances of this unity found expression at the Oxford Co-operative Congress of 1882, when Arnold Toynbee urged co-operators to undertake the education of the citizen. By this he meant: "the education of each member of the community as regards the relation in which he stands to other individual citizens and to the community as a whole." "We have abandoned," he said further, "and rightly abandoned the attempt to realise citizenship by separating ourselves from society. We will never abandon the belief that it has yet to be won amid the stress and confusion of the ordinary world in which we move." From that day to this co-operators have always had before them an ideal of education in citizenship and have organised definite teaching year by year.

Another instance of even greater power lies in the co-operation between the pioneers of the University Extension Movement at Cambridge and the working men, particularly of Rochdale and Nottingham, to be followed later by that unprecedented revival of learning amongst working people which took place in Northumberland and Durham in the days before the great coal strike. At a later date, in 1903, the same kind of united action gave rise to the movement of the Workers' Educational Association, which has always conceived its purpose to be the development of citizenship in and through education pursued in common by university man and working man alike. The system of University Tutorial Classes originated by this Association has been based upon an ideal of citizenship, and not primarily upon a determination to acquire knowledge, although it was clearly seen that vague aspirations towards good citizenship without the harnessing of all available knowledge to its cause would be futile. After exception has been made for the body of young men and women who are determined to acquire technical education for the laudable purpose of advancing both their position in life and their utility to society, it is clear that no educational appeal to working men and women will have the least effect if it is not directed towards the purpose of enriching their life, and through them the life of the community. The proof of this lies in the fact that, after they have striven together for years in Tutorial Classes, they ask for no recognition—in fact they have declined it when it has been offered—and have devoted their powers to voluntary civic work and the work of the associations or unions to which they belong, as well as in very many instances, to the spreading of education throughout the districts in which they live. It is largely due to the leaven of educational enthusiasm which has thus been generated that there is a unanimous movement on the part of working people towards a complete educational system including within it compulsory attendance at continuation schools during the day.

The problems that hedge about continuation schools are many, but it is clear that they will be regarded by educationists and by at least some employers as above all else training for citizenship based upon the vocation to which the boy or girl may be devoting himself or herself in working hours. The narrowness of the daily occupation, divorced as it is from the whole spirit and intent of apprenticeship, will be broadened directly the consideration of daily work is placed in the continuation school both on a higher plane and in a complete setting.

The compulsory evening school will fail unless it induces a demand for recreation of a pure kind which may be associated with the voluntary evening school and continued along the lines of study into the years of adult life. And even if it is impossible for every student of capacity in the continuation school to pass into the university or technological college, it may be hoped that there need not fail to be opportunities for reaching the heights of ascertained knowledge in the University Tutorial Class. In the future, as now, only in greater degree, such classes will be regarded as an essential part of university work, and will provide opportunity for the study of those subjects which are most nearly related to citizenship.

It is one of the fundamental principles of the Workers' Educational Association that every person, when not under the power of some hostile over-mastering influence, is ready to respond to an educational appeal. Not indeed that all are ready or able to become scholars, but that all are anxious to look with understanding eyes at the things which are pure and beautiful. Tired men and women are made better citizens if they are taken, as they often are, to picture galleries and museums, to places of historic interest and of scenic beauty, and are helped to understand them by the power of a sympathetic guide. It is by the extension of work of this sort, which can be carried out almost to a limitless extent, that the true purpose of social reform will be best served. It is by such means that the press may be elevated, the level of the cinema raised, the efforts of the demagogue neutralised.

The Workers' Educational Association is based upon the work of the elementary school and of the associations of working people, notably the co-operative societies and trade unions. The democratic methods obtaining in those associations have themselves proved a valuable contribution to citizenship, and have determined the democratic nature of all adult education. The right and freedom of the student to study what he wishes finds its counterpart in the reasonable demand that man shall live out his life as he wills, provided it moves in a true direction and is in harmony with the needs and aspirations of his fellows.

It has seemed in this review of the relation of schools and places of education to the development of citizenship that the fact of the operation of social influences has been implicit at every point. In any case there is, and can be, no doubt that the school, whilst instant in its effect upon the mind of the time, is always being either hindered or helped by the conditions obtaining in the society in which it is set. The relations existing between society and school are revealed in a process of action and reaction. Wilhelm von Humboldt said that "whatever we wish to see introduced into the life of a nation must first be introduced into its schools." Among other things, it is necessary to develop in the schools an appreciation of all work that is necessary for human welfare. This is the crux of all effort towards citizenship through education. In the long run there can be no full citizenship unless there is fulness of intention to discover capacity and to develop it not for the individual but for the common good. This is primarily the task of an educational system. If a man is set to work for which he is not fitted, whether it be the work of a student or a miner, he is thwarted in his innate desire to attain to the full expression of his being in and through association with his fellow-men, whereas, when a man is doing the right work, that for which he has capacity, he rejoices in his labour and strives continually to perfect it by development of all his powers. The exercise of good citizenship follows naturally as the inevitable result of a rightly developed life. It may not be the citizenship which is exercised by taking active and direct part in methods of government. The son of Sirach, meditating on the place of the craftsman, said:

All these trust to their hands: and every one is wise in his work. Without these cannot a city be inhabited...they will maintain the state of the world, and all their desire is in the work of their craft[1].

The times are different and the needs of people have changed, but the true test of a citizen may be more in the healthiness of dominating purpose than

[1] *Ecclesiasticus*, xxxviii. 31—34.

in the possession and satisfaction of a variety of desires. To "maintain the state of the world" is no mean ambition.

If it is difficult for a man to become the good citizen when employed on work for which he is unfitted, it is even more difficult for the man to do so who is set to shoddy work or to work which damages the community.

The task laid upon the school is heavy, but it does not stand alone. The family and the Church are its natural allies in the modern State.

All alike will make mistakes, but, if they clearly set before them the intention to do their utmost to free the capacity of all for the accomplishment of the good of all, wisdom will increase and many tragedies in life will be averted.

Thus lofty ideals have presented themselves, but they will secure universal admission apart from the immediate practical considerations which bulk so largely and often so falsely in the minds of men, and which are frequently suggested by limitations of finance and lack of faith in the all-sufficient power of wisdom.

It is in the consecration of a people to its highest ideals that the true city and the true State become realised on earth and the measure of its consecration, in spite of all devices of teaching or training however wise, determines the true level of citizenship at any time in any place.

SOME BOOKS ON CITIZENSHIP

*American Political Science Assoc. The Teaching of Government. 1916. Macmillan. 5s. od. net.

*BAKER, J. H. Educational Aims and Civic Needs. 1913. Longmans. 3s. 6d. net.

*BALCH, G. T. The Method of Teaching Patriotism in Public Schools. 1890. New York: Van Nostrand.

*BOURNE, H. E. The Teaching of History and Civics. 1915. Longmans. 6s. od. net.

*DEWEY, JOHN. Democracy and Education. 1916. Macmillan. 6s. od. net.

*DEWEY JOHN. The School and Society. 1915. Chicago Univ. Press. 4s. od. net.

*DEWEY, JOHN and EVELYN. Schools of To-Morrow. 1915. Dent. 5s. od. net.

FINDLAY, J. J. The School. 1912. Williams and Norgate. 1s. 3d. net.

*HALL, G. STANLEY. Educational Problems. 2 vols. 1911. Appleton. 31s. 6d. net. Ch. 24. Civic Education.

*HENDERSON, C. H. Education and the Larger Life. 1902. Boston: Houghton. 6s. od.

*HUGHES, E. H. The Teaching of Citizenship. 1909. Boston: Wilde. 6s. od.

HUGHES, M. L. V. Citizens To Be. 1915. Constable. 4s. 6d. net.

*JENKS, J. W. Citizenship and the Schools. 1909. New York: Holt. 6s. od.

KERSCHENSTEINER, GEORG. Education for Citizenship. Tr. A. J. Pressland. 1915. Harrap. 2s. od. net.

—— The Schools and the Nation. 1914. Macmillan. 6s. od. net.

*MONROE, PAUL. (Ed.) Cyclopedia of Education. 5 vols. Macmillan. 105s. od. net.

MORGAN, ALEXANDER. Education and Social Progress. 1916. Longmans. 3s. 6d. net.

Oxford and Working Class Education. Clarendon Press. 1s. net.

PATERSON, ALEXANDER.. Across the Bridges. 1912. Arnold. 1s. od. net.

SADLER, M. E. (Ed.). Continuation Schools in England and Elsewhere. 1908. Manchester University Press. 8s. 6d. net.

*SCOTT, C. A. Social Education. 1908. Ginn. 6s. od. net.

WALLAS, GRAHAM. The Great Society. 1914. Macmillan. 7s. 6d. net.

See also:

Board of Education. Reports.

Civics and Moral Education League Papers, 6 York Buildings, Adelphi, W.C. 2.

* American.

VI

THE PLACE OF LITERATURE IN EDUCATION

By NOWELL SMITH
Head Master of Sherborne School

Education is a subject upon which everyone—or at least every parent—considers himself entitled to have opinions and to express them. But educational treatises or the considered views of educational experts have a very limited popularity, and in fact arouse little interest outside the circle of the experts themselves. Even the average teacher, who is himself, if only he realised it, inside the circle, pays little heed to the broader aspects of education, chiefly, no doubt, because in the daily practice of the art of education he cannot step aside and see it as a whole; he cannot see the wood for the trees. The indifference of laymen however is mainly due to the fact that educational theory, like other special subjects, inevitably acquires a jargon of its own, an indispensable shorthand, as it were, for experts, but far too abstract and technical for outsiders.

And his technical language too often reacts upon the actual ideas of the educational theorist, who tends to lose sight of the variety of concrete boys and girls in his abstract reasonings, necessary as these are. We are apt to forget that what is sauce for the goose may not be sauce for the gander, and still more perhaps that what is sauce for the swan may not be sauce for either of these humbler but deserving fowl. But it is certain that in discussing education we ought constantly to envisage the actual individuals to be educated. Otherwise our "average pupil of fifteen plus" is only too likely to become a mere monster of the imagination, and the intellectual *pabulum*, which we propose to offer, suited to the digestion of no human boy or girl in "this very world, which is the world of all of us."

In considering, then, the place of literature in education, I propose to keep constantly before my eyes the people with whose education I am personally familiar, namely, myself, my children, and the various types of public school boy which I have known as boy, as undergraduate, as college tutor and as schoolmaster. I say various types of public school boy; for although there still is a public school type in general which is easily recognisable by certain marked superficial characteristics, the popular notion that all public school boys are very much alike in character and outlook is a mere delusion

Again, I propose, when I speak of literature, to mean literature, and not a compendious term for anything that is not science. The opposition that has in modern times been set up between science on the one hand and a jumble of studies labelled either literary

or "humanistic" studies on the other is to my mind
wholly unfounded in the nature of things, and destructive of any liberal view of education. It may
perhaps be held that literature in its most literal sense
is a name for anything that is expressed by means of
intelligible language—a use of the word which certainly admits of no comparison with the meaning of
science, but which also leads to no ideas of any educational interest. But I take the word literature in its
common acceptation; and, while admitting that I can
give no precise and exhaustive definition, I will venture
to describe it as the expression of thought or emotion
in any linguistic forms which have aesthetic value.
Thus the subject-matter of literature is only limited
by experience: as Emile Faguet says somewhere—
without claiming to have made a discovery—*la littérature est une chose qui touche à toutes choses.* And
the tones of literature range from Isaiah to Wycherley,
from Thucydides to Tolstoy; its forms from Pindar
to a folk song, from Racine to Rudyard Kipling, from
Gibbon to Herodotus or Froissart. And while no two
people would agree in drawing the line of aesthetic
value which should determine whether any given
verbal expression of thought or emotion was literature
or not—a fact which is not without importance in
the choice of books for forming the taste of our pupils
—yet, for the purpose of discussing the place and
function of literature in education, we all know well
enough what we mean by the word in the general
sense which I have attempted to describe.

As this is not a tractate on education as a whole,

I must risk something for the sake of brevity, and will venture to lay down dogmatically that the objects of literary studies as a part of education are (1) the formation of a personality fitted for civilised life, (2) the provision of a permanent source of pure and inalienable pleasure, and (3) the immediate pleasure of the student in the process of education. None of these objects is exclusive of either of the others. They cannot in fact be separated in the concrete. But they are sufficiently different to be treated distinctly.

(1) Hardly anyone would deny that some knowledge and appreciation of literature is an indispensable part of a complete education. The full member of a civilised society must be able to subscribe to the familiar *Homo sum ; nihil humanum a me alienum puto.* And literature is obviously one of the greatest, most intense, and most prolific interests of humanity. There have always been thinkers, from Plato downwards, who for moral or political reasons have viewed the power of literature with distrust: but their fear is itself evidence of that power. Thus literature is a very important part both of the past and of contemporary life, and no one can enter fully into either without some real knowledge of it. A man may be a very great man or a very good man without any literary culture; he may do his country and the world imperishable services in peace or war. But the older the world grows, the rarer must these unlettered geniuses become. Literature in one form or another—too often no doubt put to vile uses—has become so much part of the very texture of civilised life that a wide-awake

mind can scarcely fail to take notice of it. And in any case we need not consider that kind of special genius which education does little either to make or mar. No one is likely seriously to deny that for taking a full and intelligent part in the normal life of a civilised community—in love and friendship, in the family and in society, in the study and practice of citizenship of all degrees—some literary culture is absolutely necessary; nor indeed that, subject to a due balance of qualities and acquirements, the wider and deeper the literary culture the more valuable a member of society the possessor will be. The lubricant of society in all its functions, whether of business or leisure, is sympathy, and a sufficient quantity, as it were, of sympathy to lubricate the complex mechanism of civilised life can only be supplied by a widespread knowledge of the best, and a great deal more than the best, of what has been and is being thought and said in the world. Personal intercourse with one another and a common apprehension of God as our Father are even more powerful sources of sympathy; but literature provides innumerable channels for the intercommunication and distribution of these sources, without which the sympathies of individuals may be strong and lively, but will almost always be narrowly circumscribed. It is very true that to know mankind only through books is no knowledge of mankind at all; but ever since man discovered how to perpetuate his utterances in writing it has been increasingly true that literature is the principal means of widening and deepening such knowledge.

This object of literary studies, the formation of a personality fitted for civilised life, may be summed up in the familiar graceful words of Ovid, who was thinking almost entirely of literature when he wrote

> ingenuas didicisse fideliter artes
> Emollit mores nec sinit esse feros.

And it is only the lack, in so many of the greatest writers, and the neglect, in so many educators and educational systems, of that due balance of qualities and acquirements of which I spoke just now, which have induced in superficial minds a distrust and often a contempt of literature as a subject of education. The good citizen or man of the world—in the best sense of the phrase—must not be the slave of literary proclivities to the ruin of his functions as father or husband or friend or man of action and affairs. The world of letters, if lived in too exclusively, is an unreal world, though without it the actual world is almost meaningless. Now the *genus irritabile vatum*, even when their thoughts, as Carlyle put it, "enrich the blood of the world," have very generally appeared to the plain man of goodwill as very defective in the art of living. If their aspirations have been above the standards of their day, their practice has often been below them in such essentially social qualities as probity, faithfulness, consideration for others. Moreover their outlook upon life, intense and inspiring though it be, is often a very partial one. Even so, it does not follow that because a poet or a philosopher is not in every respect "the compleat gentleman," a citizen *totus teres atque rotundus*, his works are not profitable for the building up of that character. If it did, we must by parity of reasoning discard the discoveries of a misanthropic inventor and the theories of a bigamous chemist. We go to Plato and Catullus, to Shakespeare and Shelley, for what they have to give: if we go with our own pet notions of what that ought to be, we are naturally as disgusted as Herbert Spencer was with Homer and Tolstoy with Shakespeare. Tolstoy is indeed a case in point. He is one of the giants of literature, whose masterpieces are already classics; and this position is unaffected by the various judgments that may be formed either of his critical or of his practical wisdom.

The lack then of a due balance of qualities and acquirements in so many authors, and we may add other artists, is a cause, but no justification, of that belittlement and even distrust of the literary side of education which are on the whole marked features of the English attitude to-day. But a more potent cause and a real justification of this attitude is the neglect of due balance of qualities and acquirements by so many educators and educational systems. Great educators have themselves rarely been narrow-minded men; but the traditions they have founded have gone the way of all traditions.

What begins as an inspiration hardens into a formula. The ideals of the Renascence were caricatured in their offspring of the eighteenth and nineteenth centuries. Not only did the evolution of modern life with its cities, its printing press, its gunpowder, its steam engine and the rest, destroy the need of the well-to-do to be trained in the practical arts of chivalry, of the chase, of husbandry, even of music and design, so that the bodily activities of boys became relegated to the sphere of mere games and pastimes; but as books usurped more and more of the hours of boyhood, so the instructors of youth fell more and more into the fatally easy path of formal and grammatical treatment. The subject-matter of education was indeed literature, and the very noblest literatures, mainly those of Greece and Rome: but there was little of literary or humane interest about the study of it; its meaning and spirit were concealed from all but the few who could surmount the fences of linguistic pedantry and artificial technique with which it was surrounded.

I do not know when the expression "the dead languages" was invented: but certainly Latin and Greek have been treated as very dead languages by the great majority of teachers for a very long time. And as "modern subjects," history, geography, modern languages and literatures, gradually thrust their way into the curriculum, each was subjected as far as possible to the same mummification. There is a theory still widely held among teachers that the value of a subject or of a method of instruction depends upon the amount of drudgery which it involves or the degree of repulsion which it excites. The theory rests upon a confusion between the ideas of discipline and punishment, which itself is probably due to the strongly Judaistic tone of our so-called Christianity.

At any rate, far too many schoolmasters suffer from conscientious scruples about allowing the spirits of freedom, initiative, curiosity, enjoyment, to blow through their class-rooms.

There has been, always to some extent, but with gathering force in recent years, a natural revolt against this mixture of puritanism, scholasticism, and dilettantism, which made the intellectual side of public school education such a failure except for the few who were born with the spoon of scholarship in their mouths. The irruption of that turbulent rascal, natural science, has perhaps had most to do with humanising our humanistic studies. It was a great step when boys who could not make verses were allowed to make if it was but a smell; and even breaking a test-tube once in a while is more educative than breaking the gender-rules every day of the week. Many of my friends, who label themselves humanists, are in a panic about this, and look upon me sadly as a renegade because I, who owe almost everything to a "classical education," am ready (they think) to sell the pass of "compulsory Greek" to a horde of money-grubbing barbarians who will turn our flowery groves of Academe into mere factories of commercial efficiency. But fear is a treacherous guide. They are the victims of that abstract generalisation of which I spoke at the outset. I check their forebodings by reference to concrete personalities, myself, my children, and the hundreds of boys I have known. And I see more and more plainly, as I study the infinite variety of our mental lineaments and the common stock of human nature and civilised society which unites us, that literature is a permanent and indispensable and even inevitable element in our education; and that moreover it can only have free scope and growth in the expanding personality of the young in a due and therefore a varying harmony with other interests. I and my children and my schoolboys have eyes and ears and hands—and even legs! We have, as Aristotle rightly saw, an appetite for knowledge, and that appetite cannot be satisfied, though it may be choked, by a sole diet of literature. We have desires of many kinds demanding satisfaction and requiring government. We have a sense of duty and vocation: we know that we and our families must eat to live and to carry on the race. We resent, in our inarticulate way, these sneers at our Philistinism, commercialism, athleticism, materialism, from dim-eyed pedants on the one hand and superior persons on the other, who have evidently forgotten, if they ever saw, the whole purport of that Greek literature the name of which they take in vain. No! *La littérature est une chose qui touche à toutes choses*; but if we are to shut our eyes to all the "things" which evoke it, it becomes what it is to so many, whose education has been in name predominantly literary, "a tale told by an idiot, full of sound and fury, signifying nothing."

(2) The argument has already insensibly led us to treat by implication the second, and indeed the third of our assumed objects. But in our modern insistence upon social relations and citizenship—a very proper insistence, still too much warped and hampered

by selfishness and prejudice—there is a real danger of our forgetting how much of our conscious existence is passed, in a true sense, at leisure and alone. It is our ideal on the one side to be "all things to all men": and for any approach to this ideal, as we have seen, the knowledge and sympathy born of literature are indispensable. But on the other side no man or woman is completely fitted out without provision for the blank spaces, the passages and waiting rooms, as it were, to say nothing of the actual "recreation rooms" of the house of life. And there is no provision so abundant, so accessible to all, so permanent, so independent of fortune, and at once so mellowing and fortifying, as literature. Our happiness or discontent depends far more, than on anything else, on the habitual occupation of our mind when it is free to choose its occupation. And, since thought is instantaneous, even the busiest of us has far more of that freedom than he knows what to do with unless he has a mental treasury from which he can at will bring forth things new and old. It is impossible to exaggerate the importance of hobbies in a man's own life— and of course indirectly in his relations with his fellows. A single hobby is dangerous. You ride it to death or it becomes your master. You need at least a pair of them in the stable. What they are must depend, you say, upon the temperament, the bent of the individual. True: but our main responsibility as educators consists in our "bending of the twig." It is not temperament nor destiny which renders so many men and women unable to fill their leisure moments with anything more exhilarating than gossip, grumbling, or perpetual bridge. Perhaps the greatest blessing which a parent or a teacher can confer on a boy or girl is discreet, unpriggish, and unpatronising, encouragement and guidance in the discovery and development of hobbies: and if I may venture on a piece of advice to anyone who needs it, I should say: "Try to secure that everyone grows up with at least two hobbies; and whatever one of them may be, let the other be literature, or some branch of literature."

> Dreams, books, are each a world ; and books, we know,
> Are a substantial world, both pure and good ;
> Round these, with tendrils strong as flesh and blood,
> Our pastime and our happiness will grow.

(3) At this point I can imagine someone, who recognises the importance of literary culture in the equipment of a man or woman of the world, and perhaps feels even more strongly the truth summed up in these lines of Wordsworth, expressing the doubt whether the second at least of these objects can be secured, or will not rather be precluded, by admitting the study of literature as such into the school curriculum. This doubt, which I have heard expressed by many lovers of literature, notably by the late Canon Ainger, is not lightly to be disregarded. It is to be met, however, in my opinion, by keeping clearly before our eyes the third of the objects which we assumed to be aimed at by literary studies as a branch of education —the immediate pleasure of the student. The two objects which we have already discussed are ulterior

objects, which should be part of the fundamental faith of the teacher; but while the teacher is in contact with his pupils they should be forgotten in the glowing conviction that the study of literature is, at that very moment, the most delightful thing in the world. Of course we all know, or should know, that this is the only attitude of mind for the best teaching in any subject whatever. It takes a great deal more than enthusiasm to make a competent teacher; and it is easy to prepare pupils successfully for almost any written examination without any enthusiasm for anything except success. But, cramming apart, a bored teacher is inevitably a boring one: and while unfortunately the converse is not universally true and an enthusiastic teacher may fail to communicate his enthusiasm, yet it is quite certain that you cannot communicate enthusiasm if you are not possessed of it.

But this enthusiasm, indispensable for the best teaching of anything, is, so to speak, doubly indispensable for even competent teaching of literature. On the one hand the ulterior objects of the study, of which I have tried to indicate the importance, are of an impalpable kind. I doubt if there is any subject of the curriculum which it would be so difficult to commend to an uninterested pupil by an appeal to simple utilitarian motives. On the other hand there clings to literature, and particularly to poetry, which is the quintessence of literature, an air of pleasure-seeking, of holiday, of irresponsibility and detachment from the work-a-day world, which must captivate the student, or else the study itself will seem very poor fooling compared with football or hockey. If the attitude of the teacher reflects the old question of the Latin Grammar "Why should I teach you letters?" he would better turn to some other subject which his pupils will more easily recognise as appropriate to school hours.

> What's Hecuba to him, or he to Hecuba,
> That he should weep for her—

unless indeed he be a candidate for Responsions?

"Ah! it is just as I expected," says my friend Orbilius at this point: "this literature-lesson of yours is to be mere play, a 'soft-option' for our modern youth, who is not to be made to stand up to the tussle with Latin prose or riders in geometry." Softly, my friend! It is quite true that those twin engines of education, classics and mathematics, are adapted partly by long practice, but partly, as I too believe, by their very nature, to discipline the youthful mind to habits of intellectual honesty, of accuracy, of industry and perseverance. It is true that they accomplish some of this discipline—though at what a cost! —in the hands of indifferent teachers. It is true that every other subject of the usual curriculum is much more obviously liable than they are to the dangers of idleness, unreality, false pretence; and that the scoffs, for instance, about "playing with test-tubes," "tracing maps," "dishing up history notes," are in fact too often deserved. But in the first place, if the object to be attained is a worthy one, it is our business to face the dangers of the road, and not to give up the object. If a knowledge and love of literature is part of the

birthright of our children, and a part which, as things
are, very many of them will never obtain away from
school, then we teachers must strive to give it them,
even if the process seems shockingly frivolous to the
grammarian or the geometrician. And, secondly, it
is not true that the study of literature, even in the
mother tongue, cannot be a discipline and a delight
together. The two are very far from incompatible:
indeed that discipline is most effective which is almost
or quite unconsciously self-imposed in the joyous
exercise of one's own faculties. The genuine foot-
baller and the genuine scholar will both agree with
Ferdinand the lover, that

> There be some sports are painful, and their labour
> Delight in them sets off.

And the "labour" of the boy or girl who is really
wrapped up in a play of Shakespeare or is striving to
express the growing sense of beauty in fitting forms
of language, is no less truly spiritual discipline because
it is felt not as pain but as interest and delight.

It is fortunately no part of my business to endeavour
to instruct teachers in the methods of imparting the
love and knowledge of literature. But the value of
literary studies in education depends so much upon
the spirit in which they are pursued that I may perhaps
be permitted a few more words on the practical side of
the subject. I have already repeated the truism that
no one can impart enthusiasm who is not himself possessed of it: but even the lover of literature sometimes
lacks that clear consciousness of aim, and that sympathetic understanding of the personality of his pupil,

which are both essential to successful teaching. Just as the clever young graduate is tempted to dictate his own admirable history notes to a class of boys, or to puzzle them with the latest theories in archaeology or philosophy, so the literary teacher is apt to dazzle his pupils with brilliant but to them unintelligible criticism, or to surfeit them with literary history, or to impose upon them an inappropriate literary diet because it happens to suit his maturer taste or even his caprice. No one is likely to deny that such errors are possible; but I should not venture to speak so decidedly, if I were not aware of having too often fallen into them myself. And the only safeguard for the teacher is the familiar "Keep your eye on the object"—and that in a double sense. We must have a clear conception of our aim, and also a living sympathy with our pupils. I have attempted to indicate the aim, the equipment of boy or girl for civilised life and for spiritual enjoyment. It will be sympathy with our pupils which will chiefly dictate both the method and the material of our instruction. In the early stages of education this sympathy is generally to be found either in parents, if they are fond of literature, or in the teacher, who is usually of the more sympathetic sex. The stories and poetry offered to children nowadays seem to be, as a rule, sympathetically, if sometimes rather uncritically, chosen. The importance of voice and ear in receiving the due impression of literature is recognised; and the value of the child's own expression of its imaginations and its sense of rhythm and assonance is understood.

Probably more teachers than Mr Lamborn supposes would heartily subscribe to the faith which glows in his delightful little book *The Rudiments of Criticism*, though there must be very few who would not be stimulated by reading it.

It is when we come to the middle stage, at any rate of boyhood—for of girls' schools I am not qualified to speak—that there is a good deal to be done before the cultivation of literary taste, and all that this carries with it, will be successfully pursued. In the past, the Latin and Greek classics were, for the few who really absorbed them, both a potent inspiration and an unrivalled discipline in taste: but it is noteworthy how few even of the *élite* acquired and retained that lively and generous love of literature which would have enabled them to sow seeds of the divine fire far and wide—"of joy in widest commonalty spread." Considering the intensity with which the classics have been studied in the old universities and public schools of the United Kingdom, the fine flower of scholarship achieved, the sure touch of style and criticism, one cannot help being amazed at the low standard of literary culture in the rank and file of the classes from which this *élite* has been drawn. How rare has been the power, or even apparently the desire, of a Bradley or a Verrall or a Murray, to carry the flower of their classical culture into the fields of modern literary study! And how few and fumbling the attempts of ordinary classical teachers to train their pupils in the appreciation of our English literature!

In recent years a new type of literary teachers has been rising, who owe little, at any rate directly, to the old classical training; and although their zeal is often undisciplined and "not according to knowledge," with them lies the future hope of literary training in our schools. They bring to their task an enthusiasm which was too often lacking in the "grand old fortifying classical curriculum"; but it is to be hoped that, as the importance of their subject becomes more and more recognised, they will achieve a method which will embody all that was valuable, while discarding much that was narrow and pedantic, in classical teaching. And in particular may they all realise, as many already do, what the classical teacher, however unconsciously, held as an axiom, that in order to enter into the spirit of literature, to appreciate style, to understand in any true sense the meaning of great authors, it is not enough for pupils to listen and to read, and then perhaps to write essays about what they have heard and read. They must also *make* something, exercise that creative, and at the same time imitative, artistic faculty, which surely is the motive power of most of our progress, at least in early life. Nothing has struck me more forcibly than the intense interest which boys will take in their own crude efforts at writing a poem or a story or essay, while they are still quite unable to appreciate with discrimination, or even to enjoy with any sustained feeling, the poetry or prose of the great masters. Not that there is anything surprising in this. I know very well that it was writing Latin verses that taught me to appreciate

Virgil, and writing juvenile epics that led me up to Milton. But it is an order of progress which we schoolmasters are apt to overlook, expecting our pupils to appreciate what we know to be good work before they have that elementary, but most fruitful, experience which can only come from handling the tools of the craft. The creative and imitative impulse will die down in the great majority; and we shall not make the mistake of continuing to exact formal "composition" from maturer pupils, who no longer find it anything but a drag upon their progress along the unfolding vistas of knowledge and appreciation. Our object is not to increase the number of writers, already far too large, but to increase the number of readers, which can never be too large, to raise the standard of literary taste, and so to spread pure enjoyment and all the benefits to society which joy, and joy alone, confers. Inspired with such an aim, common sense and sympathy will enable us to overcome the difficulties and avoid the pitfalls which undoubtedly beset the teaching of that most necessary, most delightful, but most elusive and imponderable subject, the appreciation of literature.

VII

THE PLACE OF SCIENCE IN EDUCATION

By W. BATESON

Director of the John Innes Horticultural Institution

That secondary education in England fails to do what it might is scarcely in dispute. The magnitude of the failure will be appreciated by those who know what other countries accomplish at a fraction of the cost. Beyond the admission that something is seriously wrong there is little agreement. We are told that the curriculum is too exclusively classical, that the classes are too large, the teaching too dull, the boys too much away from home, the examination-system too oppressive, athletics overdone. All these things are probably true. Each cause contributes in its degree to the lamentable result. Yet, as it seems to me, we may remove them all without making any great improvement. All the circumstances may be varied, but that intellectual apathy which has become so marked a characteristic of English life, especially of English public and social life, may not improbably continue. Why nations pass into these morbid phases no one can tell. The spirit of the age, that "polarisation of society" as Tarde[1] used to call it, in a definite direction, is brought about by no cause that can be named as yet. It will remain beyond volitional control at least until we get some real insight into social physiology. That the attitude or pose of the average Englishman towards education, knowledge, and learning is largely a phenomenon of infectious imitation we know. But even if we could name the original, perhaps real, perhaps fictional, person—for in all likelihood there was such an one—whom English society in its folly unconsciously selected as a model, the knowledge would advance us little. The psychology of imitation is still impenetrable and likely to remain so. The simple interpretation of our troubles as a form of sloth—a travelling along lines of least resistance—can scarcely be maintained. For first there have been times when learning and science were the fashion. Whether society benefited directly therefrom may, in passing, be doubted, but certainly learning did. Secondly there are plenty of men who under the pressure of fashion devote much effort to the improvement of their form in fatuous sports, which otherwise applied would go a considerable way in the improvement of their minds and in widening their range of interests.

Of late things have become worse. In the middle of the nineteenth century a perfunctory and superficial acquaintance with recent scientific discovery was not unusual among the upper classes, and the scientific world was occasionally visited even by the august.

[1] *Les Lois de l'Imitation*, 1911, p. 87.

These slender connections have long since withered away. This decline in the public estimation of science and scientific men has coincided with a great increase both in the number of scientific students and in the provision for teaching science. It has occurred also in the period during which something of the full splendour and power of science has begun to be revealed. Great regions of knowledge have been penetrated by the human mind. The powers of man over nature have been multiplied a hundredfold. The fate of nations hangs literally on the issue of contemporary experiments in the laboratory; but those who govern the Empire are quite content to know nothing of all this. Intercommunication between government departments and scientific advisers has of course much developed. That, even in this country, was inevitable. Otherwise the Empire might have collapsed long since. Experts in the sciences are from time to time invited to confer with heads of Departments and even Cabinet Ministers, explaining to them, as best they may, the rudiments of their respective studies, but such occasional night-school talks to the great are an inadequate recognition of the position of science in a modern State. Science is not a material to be bought round the corner by the dram, but the one permanent and indispensable light in which every action and every policy must be judged.

To scientific men this is so evident that they are unable to imagine what the world looks like to other people. They cannot realise that by a majority of even the educated classes the phenomena of nature and the affairs of mankind are still seen through the old screens of mystery and superstition. The man of science regards nature as in great and ever increasing measure a soluble problem. For the layman such inquiries are either indifferent and somewhat absurd, or, if they attract his attention at all, are interesting only as possible sources of profit. I suspect that the distinction between these two classes of mind is not to any great degree a product of education.

It is contemporary commonplace that if science were more prominent in our educational system everybody would learn it and things would come all right. That interest in science would be extended is probable. There is in the population a residuum of which we will speak later, who would profit by the opportunity; but that the congenitally unscientific, the section from which the heads of government temporal and spiritual, the lawyers, administrators, politicians, the classes upon whose minds the public life of this country almost wholly depends, would by imbibition of scientific diet at any period of life, however early, be essentially altered seems in a high degree unlikely. Of the converse case we have long experience, and I would ask those who entertain such sanguine expectations, whether the results of administering literature to scientific boys give much encouragement to their views. This consideration brings us to the one hard, physiological fact that should form the foundation of all educational schemes: the congenital diversity of the individual types. Education has too long been regarded as a kind of cookery: put in such and such ingredients in given proportions and a definite product will emerge. But living things have not the uniformity which this theory of education assumes. Our population is a medley of many kinds which will continue hetero-geneous, to whatever system of education they are submitted, just as various types of animals maintain their several characteristics though nourished on identical food, or as you may see various sorts of apples remaining perfectly distinct though grafted on the same stock. Their diversity is congenital.

According to the proposal of the reformers the natural sciences should be universally taught and be given "capital importance" in the examinations for the government services, but, cordially as we may approve the suggestion, we ought to consider what exactly its adoption is likely to effect. The intention of the proposal is doubtless that our public servants, especially the highest of them, shall, while preserving the great qualities they now possess, add also a knowledge of science and especially scientific habits of mind. Such is the "ample proposition that hope makes." Does experience of men accord with it at all? Education, whether we like it or not, is a selective agency. I doubt whether the change proposed will sensibly alter the characters of the group on whom our choice at present falls. Rather, if forced upon an unwilling community, must it act by substituting another group. The most probable result would not be that the type of men who now fill great positions would become scientific, but rather that their places would be taken by men of an altogether distinct mental type. At the present time these two types of men meet but little. They scarcely know each other. Their differences are profound, affecting thoughts, ways of looking at things, and mental interests of every kind. If either could for a moment see the world with the vision of the other he would be amazed, but to do so he would need at least to be born again, and probably, as Samuel Butler remarked, of different parents. No doubt the abler man of either type could learn with more or less effort or unreadiness the subject-matter and principles of the other's business, but any one who has watched the habits of the two classes will perceive that for them in any real sense to exchange interests, or that either should adopt the scheme of proportion which the other assigns to the events of nature and of life, a metamorphosis well nigh miraculous must be presupposed.

The Bishop of London speaking lately on behalf of the National Mission said that nature helped him to believe in God, and as evidence for his belief referred to the fact that we are not "blown off" this earth as it rushes through space, declaring that this catastrophe had been averted because "Some one" had wrapped seventy miles of atmosphere round our planet[1]. Does any one think that the bishop's slip was in fact due to want of scientific teaching at Marlborough? His chances of knowing about Sir Isaac Newton, etc., etc., have been as good as those of many familiar with the accepted version. I would rather suppose that such sublunary problems had not

[1] Reported in *Evening Standard*, 11 Sept. 1916.

interested him in the least, and that he no more cared how we happen to stick on the earth's surface than St Paul cared how a grain of wheat or any other seed germinates beneath it, when he similarly was betrayed into an unfortunate illustration.

So too on the famous occasion—always cited in these debates—when a Home Secretary defended the Government for having permitted the importation of fats into Germany on the ground that the discovery that glycerine could be made from fat was a recent advance in chemistry, he was not showing the defects of a literary education so much as a want of interest in the problems of nature, and the subject-matter of science at large. It is to be presumed indeed that neither fats, nor glycerine, nor the dependent problem how living bodies are related to the world they inhabit, had ever before seemed to him interesting. Nor can we suppose they would, even if chemistry were substituted for Greek in Responsions.

The difficulty in obtaining full recognition for science lies deeper than this. It is a part of public opinion or taste which may well survive changes in the educational system. Blunders about science like those illustrated above are soon excused. Few think much the worse of the perpetrators, whereas a corresponding obliviousness to language, history, literature, and indeed to learning other than their own which we of the scientific fraternity have agreed to condone in our members is incompatible with public life of a high order. Both classes have their disabilities. That of the scientific side is well expressed in an incident which befell the late Professor Hales. Examining in the Little-Go *viva voce*, he asked a candidate, with reference to some line in a Greek play, what passage in Shakespeare it recalled to him, and received the answer "Please, sir, I am a mathematical man." Some, no doubt, would rather ignore gravitation. When, for example, one hears, as I did not long since, several scientific students own in perfect sincerity that they could not recall anything about Ananias and Sapphira and another, more enlightened, say that he was sure Ananias was a name for a liar though he could not tell why, one is driven to admit that ignorance of this special but not uncommon kind does imply more than inability to remember an old legend. We may be reluctant to confess the fact, but though most scientific men have some recreation, often even artistic in nature, we have with rare exceptions withdrawn from the world in which letters, history and the arts have immediate value, and simple allusions to these topics find us wanting. Of the two kinds of disability which is the more grave? Truly gross ignorance of science darkens more of a man's mental horizon, and in its possible bearing on the destinies of a race is far more dangerous than even total blindness to the course of human history and endeavour; and yet it is difficult to question the popular verdict that to know nothing of gravitation though ridiculous is venial, while to know nothing of Ananias is an offence which can never be forgiven.

That is the real difficulty. The people of this country have definitely preferred the unscientific type, holding the other virtually in contempt. Their choice may be right or wrong, but that it is reversible seems unlikely. Such revolutions in public opinion are rare events. Democracy moreover inevitably worships and is swayed by the spoken word. As inevitably, the range and purposes of science daily more and more transcend the comprehension—even the educated comprehension—of the vulgar, who will of course elevate the nimble and versatile, speaking a familiar language, above dull and inarticulate natural philosophers.

In these discussions there is a disposition to forget how very largely natural science is already included in the educational curriculum both at schools and universities. Schools subsidised by the Board of Education are obliged to provide science-teaching. The public schools have equipment, in some cases a superb equipment, for teaching at least physics and chemistry. At the newer universities there are great and vigorous schools of science. Of the old universities Cambridge stands out as a chief centre of scientific activity. In several branches of science Cambridge is without question pre-eminent. The endowments both of the university and the colleges are freely used for the advancement of the sciences. Not only in these material ways are scientific studies in no sense neglected, but the position of the sciences is recognised and even envied by those who follow other kinds of learning. The scientific schools of Cambridge form perhaps the dominant force among the resident body of the university, and except by virtue of some great increase in the endowments, it would be impossible to extend further the scientific side of Cambridge and still maintain other forms of intellectual activity in such proportion as to preserve that healthy co-ordination which is the life of a great university.

At Oxford the case is no doubt very different. The measure in which the sciences are esteemed appears only too plainly in the small proportion of Fellowships filled by men of science. Progress has nevertheless begun. At the remarkable Conference called in May, 1916, to protest against the neglect of science it was noticeable that the speakers were, in overwhelming majority, Oxford men[1].

Among the educational institutions of England there is no general neglect to provide teaching of natural science and much of the language used in reference to the problem of reform is not really in accord with fact. Probably no boy able to afford a good secondary school, certainly none able to proceed to a university, is debarred from scientific teaching merely because it does not "form an integral part" of the curriculum. This alone suffices to prove that the real cause of the deplorable neglect of science is to be sought elsewhere. The fundamental difficulty is that which has been already indicated, that public taste and judgment deliberately prefers the type known as literary, or as it might with more propriety be designated, "vocal." In the schools there is no lack

---

[1] Two Cambridge men spoke, one being Lord Rayleigh, the Chairman, and ten Oxford men, besides one originally Cambridge, for several years an Oxford professor.

of science teaching, but the small percentage of boys whose minds develop early and whose general capacity for learning and aptitude for affairs mark them out as leaders, rarely have much instinct for science, and avoid such teaching, finding it irksome and unsatisfying. These it is, who going afterwards to the universities, in preponderating numbers to Oxford, make for themselves a congenial atmosphere, disturbed only by faint ripples of that vast intellectual renascence in which the new shape of civilisation is forming. With self-complacency unshaken, they assume in due course charge of Church and State, the Press, and in general the leadership of the country. As lawyers and journalists they do our talking for us, let who will do the thinking. Observe that their strength lies in the possession of a special gift, which under the conditions of democratic government has a prodigious opportunity. Uncomfortable as the reflection may be, it is not to be denied that the countries in which science has already attained the greatest influence and recognition in public affairs are Germany and Japan, where the opinions of the ignorant are not invited. But facts must be recognised, and our government is likely to remain in the hands of those who have the gift of speech. A general substitution of scientific men for the "vocal" could scarcely be achieved, even if the change were desirable. The utmost limit of success which the conditions admit is some inoculation of scientific interest and ideas upon the susceptible members of the classes already preferred. That a large proportion of those persons are in the biological sense resistant to all such influences must be expected.   Granting however that a section, perhaps even the majority, of our βέλτιστοι may prove unamenable to the influences of science no one can doubt that under the present system of education a proportion of not unintelligent boys in practice have little option.   From earliest youth classics are offered to them as almost the sole vehicle of education.   They do sufficiently well in classics, as they probably would on any other curriculum, to justify themselves and their advisers in thinking that they have made a good beginning to which it is safer to stick.   The system has a huge momentum, and so, holding to the "great wheel" that goes up the hill, they let it draw them after.   In their protest against the monotony of the courses provided for young boys the reformers are right.   The trouble is not that science is not taught in the schools, but that in schools of the highest type, with certain exceptions, the young boys are not offered it.

Realising the determinism which modern biological knowledge has compelled us to accept, we suspect that the power of education to modify the destinies of individuals is relatively small. Abrogating larger hopes we recognise education in its two scientific aspects, as a selective agency, but equally as a provision of opportunity.   In view therefore of the congenital diversity of the individual types, that provision should be as diverse and manifold as possible, and the very first essential in an adequate scheme of education is that to the minds of the young something of everything should be offered, some part of all the kinds of intellectual sustenance in which the minds of men have grown and rejoiced. That should be the ideal. Nothing of varied stimulus or attraction that can be offered should be withheld. So only will the young mind discover its aptitudes and powers. This ideal education should bring all into contact with *beauty* as seen first in literature, ancient and modern, with the great models of art and the patterns of nobility of thought and of conduct; and no less should it show to all the *truth* of the natural world, the changeless systems of the universe, as revealed in astronomy or in chemistry, something too of the truth about life, what we animals really are, what our place and what our powers, a truth ungarbled whether by prudery or mysticism.

But presented with this ideal the schoolmaster will reply that something of everything means nothing *thorough*. I know the objection and what it commonly stands for. It is the cloak and pretext for that accursed pedantry and cant which turns every sort of teaching to a blight. Thoroughness is the excuse for giving boys grammar and accidence in the name of Greek: diagrams, formulae and numerical examples in the name of science. Stripped of disguise this love of thoroughness is nothing but an indolent resolve to make things easy for the teacher, and, worse still, for the examiner. Live teaching is hard work. It demands continual freshness and a mind alert. The dullest man can hear irregular verbs, and with the book he knows whether they are said right or wrong, but to take a text and show what the passage means to the world, to reconstruct the scene and the conditions in which it was written, to show the origins and the fruits of ideas or of discoveries, demand qualities of a very different order. The plea for thoroughness may no doubt be offered in perfect sincerity. There are plenty of men, especially among those who desire the office of a pedagogue, whose field of vision is constricted to a slit. If they were painters their work would be in the slang of the day, "tight." One small group of facts they see hard and sharp, without atmosphere or value. Their own knowledge having no capacity for extension, no width or relationship to the world at large, they cannot imagine that breadth in itself may be a merit. Adepts in a petty erudition without vital antecedents or consequences, they would willingly see the world shrivel to the dimensions of their own landscape.

Anticipating here the applause of the reforming party, to avoid misapprehension let it be expressly observed that pedantry of this sort is in no sense the special prerogative of teachers of classics. We meet it everywhere. Among teachers of science the type abounds, and from the papers set in any Natural Sciences Tripos, not to speak of scholarship examinations of every kind, it would be possible to extract question after question that ought never to have been set, referring to things that need never have been taught, and knowledge that no one but a pedant would dream of carrying in his head for a week.

The splendid purpose which science serves is the

inculcation of principle and balance, not facts. There is something horrible and terrifying in the doctrine so often preached, reiterated of course by speaker after speaker at the "Neglect of Science" meeting, that science is to be preferred because of its utility. If the choice were really between dead classics and dead science, or if science is to be vivified by an infusion of commercial, utilitarian spirit, then a thousand times rather let us keep to the classics as the staple of education. They at least have no "use." At least they hold the keys to the glorious places, to the fulness of literature and to the thoughtful speech of all kindred nations, nor are they demeaned with sordid, shop-keeper utility. This was plainly in the mind of the Poet Laureate, who speaking at the meeting I have referred to, said well that "a merely utilitarian science can never win the spiritual respect of mankind." The main objection that the humanists make to the introduction of natural science as a necessary subject of education, is, he declared, that science is not spiritual, that it does not work in the sphere of ideas. He went on very properly to show how perverse is such a representation of science, but, alas, in further recommendation of science as a safe subject of instruction he added that the antagonism of science to religion is ended, and that the contest had been a passing phase. Reading this we may wonder whether we are in fairness entitled to Dr Bridges's approval. "Tastes sweet the water with such specks of earth?" Since he spoke of the "unscientific attitude" of Professor Huxley as a thing of the past, candour obliges us to insist emphatically that the struggle continues and must perpetually be renewed. Huxley was opposing the teaching of science to that of revelation. In these days the ground has shifted, and supernatural teachings make preferably their defence by an appeal to intuition and other obscure phenomena which can be trusted to defy investigation. Against all such apocryphal glosses of evidential truth science protests with equal vehemence, and were Huxley here he would treat Bergson and his allies with the same scorn and contumely that he meted out to the Bishop of Oxford on the notorious occasion to which Dr Bridges made reference. As well might we decorate our writings with Plantin title-pages, showing the author embraced by angels and inspiring muses, as recommend ourselves in these disguises.

Agnosticism is the very life and mainspring of science. Not merely as to the supernatural but as to the natural world must science believe nothing save under compulsion. Little of value has a man got from science who has not learned to be slow of faith. Those early lessons in the study of the natural world will be the best which most frankly declare our ignorance, exciting the mind to attack the unknown by showing how soon the frontier of knowledge is reached. "We don't know" should be ever in the mouth of the teacher, followed sometimes by "we may find out yet." Not merely to the investigator but to the pupil the interest of science is strongest in the growing edges of knowledge. The student should be transported thither with the briefest possible delay.

Details of those parts of science which by present means of investigation are worked out and reduced to general expressions are dull and lifeless. Many and many a boy has been repelled, gathering from what he hears in class that science is a catalogue of names and facts interminable.

In childhood he may have felt curiosity about nature and the common impulse to watch and collect, but when he begins scientific lessons he discovers too often that they relate not even to the kind of fact which nature is for him, or to the subjects of his early curiosity and wonder, but to things that have no obvious interest at all, measurements of mechanical forces, reaction-formulae, and similar materials.

All these, it is true, man has gradually accumulated with infinite labour; upon them, and of such materials has the great fabric of science been reared: but to insist that the approaches to science shall be open only to those who will surmount these gratuitous obstacles is mere perversity. Men's minds do not work in that way. How many would discover the grandeur of a Gothic building if they were prevented from seeing one until they could work out stresses and strains, date mouldings, and even perhaps cut templates? Most of us, to be sure, enjoy the cathedrals more when we acquire some such knowledge, and those who are to be architects must acquire it, but we can scarcely be astonished if beginners turn away in disgust from science presented on those terms.

It is from considerations of this kind that I am led to believe that for most boys the easiest and most attractive introduction to science is from the biological side. Admittedly chemistry is the more fundamental study, and some rudimentary chemical notions must be imparted very early, but if the framework subject-matter be animals and plants, very sensible progress in realising what science means and aims at doing will have been made before the things of daily life are left behind. These first formal lessons in science should continue and extend the boy's own attempts to find out how the world is made.

I shall be charged with running counter both to common sense and to authority in expressing paren-thetically the further conviction that, in biology at least, laboratory work is now largely overdone. Whether this is so at schools I cannot tell, but at the universities whole mornings and afternoons spent in making elaborate preparations, drawings and series of sections, are frequently wasted. These courses were devised with the highest motives. Students were to "find out everything for themselves." Generally they are doing nothing of the kind. It may have been so once, but with text-books perfected and teaching stereotyped, the more industrious are slavishly veri-fying what has been verified repeatedly, or at best acquiring manipulative skill. The rest are doing nothing whatever. They would be better employed taking a walk, devilling for some investigator, browsing in museums or libraries, or even arguing with each other. Certainly a few lessons in the use of indexes and books of reference would be far more valuable. Students of every grade must of course do some laboratory work, and all should see as much material as possible. My protest is solely against those long, torpid hours compulsorily given to labour which will lead to nothing of novelty, and serves only to teach what can be got readily in other ways. There are a few whose souls crave such employment. By all means let them follow it.

But whatever is good for maturer students, biology for schoolboys should be of a less academic cast.

The natural history of animals and plants has the obvious merit that it prolongs the inborn curiosity of youth, that its subject-matter is universally at hand, accessible in holidays and in the absence of teachers or laboratories, and best of all that through biological study the significance of science appears immediately, disclosing the true story of man's relation to the world. From natural history the transition to the other sciences, especially to chemistry and physics, is easy and again natural. In the study of life many of the fundamental conceptions of those sciences are met with on the threshold, and boys whose aptitudes are rather of the physical order will at once feel the impulse to follow nature from that aspect. Biology is the more inclusive study. A man may be a good chemist and miss the broad meaning of science altogether, being sometimes indeed more devoid of such comprehension than many a philosopher fresh from Classical Greats.

In appealing for a progress from the general to the particular I am not blind to the dangers. Biology for the young readily degenerates into a mawkish "nature-study," or all-for-the-best claptrap about adaptation, but a sure remedy is the strong tonic of agnosticism, teaching one of the best lessons science has to offer, the resolute rejection of authority.

Some take comfort in the hope that all subjects may be taught as branches of science, but the fact that must permanently postpone arrival at this educational Utopia is that a great proportion of teachers are not and can never be made scientific. Nothing proceeding from such persons will by the working of any schedule, regulation, or even Order of the Board be ever made to bear any colourable resemblance to science. Moreover as has already been indicated, there are plenty of pupils also who will flourish and probably reach their highest development taught by unscientific men, pupils whose minds would be sterilised or starved by that very nourishment which to our thinking is the more generous. Were we a homogeneous population one diet for all might be justifiable, but as things are, we should offer the greatest possible variety.

From Rousseau onwards educationists, deriving their views, I suppose, from some metaphysical or theological conception of human equality, speak continually of the "mind of the child" as if the young of our species conformed to a single type. If the general spread of biological knowledge serves merely to expose that foolish assumption there would be progress to record. Dr Blakeslee[1], a well-known

---

[1] *Journ. of Heredity*, VIII. 1917, p. 53.

American biologist, lately gave a good illustration of this. In a paper on education he showed photographs of two varieties of maize. The ripe fruits of both are colourless if their sheaths be unbroken. The one, if exposed to the light before ripening, by rupture of its sheath, turns red. The second, otherwise indistinguishable, acquires no red colour though uncovered to the full sun. If these maizes were two boys, not improbably the one would be caned for failing to respond to treatment so efficacious in the case of the other. When we hear that such a man has developed too exclusively one side of his nature, with what propriety do we assume that he had any other side to develop? Or when we say that such-and-such a course of study tends to make boys too exclusively literary, or scientific, or what not, do we not really mean that it provides too exclusively for those whose aptitudes are of these respective kinds? Living in the midst of a mongrel population we note the divers powers of our fellows and we thoughtlessly imagine that if something different had happened to us, we can't say what, we should have been able to rival them. A little honest examination of our powers shows how vain are such suppositions. The right course is to make some provision for all sorts, since unscientific teaching and unscientific persons will remain with us always.

Teaching of this universal and undifferentiated sort, provided for all in common, should be continued up to the age at which pupils begin to show their tastes and aptitudes, in general about 16, after which stage such latitude of choice should be given as the resources of the school can provide.

Of what should the undifferentiated teaching consist? Coming from a cultivated home a boy of 10 may be expected to have learned the rudiments of Latin, and at least one modern language, preferably French, *colloquially*, arithmetic, outlines of geography, tales from Plutarch and from other histories. Going to a preparatory school he will read easy Latin texts *with translations* and notes; French books, geography including the elements of astronomy, beginning also algebra and geometry. At 12 dropping French except perhaps a reading once a week, he will begin Greek, by means of easy passages again with the translations beside him, continuing the rest as before. Transferred at 14½ to a public school he will go on with Latin, starting Latin prose, Greek texts, again read fast with translations. He will now have his first formal introduction to science in the guise of biology, leading up to lessons and demonstrations in chemistry and physics. At about 16½ he may drop classics *or mathematics* according as his tastes have declared themselves, adding modern languages instead, continuing science in all cases, greater or less in amount according to his proclivities.

Boys with special mathematical ability will of course need special treatment. Moreover provision of German for all has avowedly not been made. For all it is desirable and for many indispensable. But as the number who read it for pleasure, never very large, seems likely to diminish, German may perhaps be reserved as a tool, the use of which must be acquired when necessary.

Such a scheme, I submit, makes no impossible demand on the time-table, allowing indeed many spare hours for accessory subjects such as readings in English or history. Note the main features of this programme. The time for things worth learning is found by dropping *grammar* as a subject of special study. There are to be no lessons in grammar or accidence as such, nor of course any verse compositions except for older boys specialising in classics. *Mathematics* also is treated as a subject which need not be carried beyond the rudiments unless mathematical or physical ability is shown. For other boys it leads literally nowhere, being a road impassable.

All the languages are to be taught as we learn them in later life, when the desire or necessity arises, by means of easy passages with the translation at our side. Our present practice not only fails to teach languages but it succeeds in teaching how *not* to learn a language. Who thinks of beginning Russian by studying the "aspects" of the verbs, or by committing to memory the 28 paradigms which German grammarians have devised on the analogy of Latin declensions? Auxiliary verbs are the pedagogue's delight, but who begins Spanish by trying to discriminate between *tener* and *haber*, or *ser* and *estar*, or who learns tables of exceptions to improve his French? These things come by use or not at all.

If languages are treated not as lessons but as vehicles of speech, and if the authors are read so that

we may find out what they say and how they say it,
and at such a pace that we follow the train of thought
or the story, all who have any sense of language at all
can attend and with pleasure too.   What chance has
a boy of enjoying an author when he knows him only
as a task to be droned through, thirty lines at a time?
Small blame to the pupil who never discovers that the
great authors were men of like passions with ourselves,
that the Homeric songs were made to be shouted at
feasts to heroes full of drink and glory, that Herodotus
is telling of wonders that his friends, and we too, want
to hear, that in the tragedies we hear the voice of
Sophocles dictating, choked with emotion and tears;
that even Roman historians wrote because they had
something to tell, and Caesar, dull proser that he is,
composed the *Commentaries* not to provide us with
style or grammatical curiosities, but as a record of
extraordinary events.   To get into touch with any
author he must be read at a good pace, and by reading
of that kind there is plenty of time for a boy before
he reaches 17 to make acquaintance with much of
the best literature both of Greek and Latin.

Education must be brought up to date; but if in
accomplishing that, we lose Greek, it will have been
sacrificed to obstinate formalism and pedagogic tradition.   The defence of classics as a basis of education is
generally misrepresented by opponents.   The unique
value of the classics is not in any begetting of literary
style.   We are thinking of readers not of writers.
Much of the best literature is the work of unlettered
men, as they never tire of telling us, but it is for the

enjoyment and understanding of books and of the world that continuity with the past should be maintained. John Bunyan wrote sterling prose, knowing no language but his own. But how much could he read? What judgments could he form? We want also to keep classics and especially Greek as the bountiful source of material and of colour, decoration for the jejune lives of common men. If classics cease to be generally taught and become the appanage of a few scholars, the gulf between the literary and the scientific will be made still wider. Milton will need more explanatory notes than O. Henry. Who will trouble about us scientific students then? We shall be marked off from the beginning, and in the world of laboratories Hector, Antigone and Pericles will soon share the fate of poor Ananias and Sapphira.

I come now to the gravest part of the whole question. We plead for the preservation of literature, especially classical literature, as the staple of education in the name of beauty and understanding: but no less do we demand science in the name of truth and advancement. Given that our demand succeeds, what consequences may we expect? Nothing immediate, as I fear. In opening the discussion it was argued that even if scientific knowledge be widely diffused, any great change in the composition of the ruling classes is scarcely attainable under present conditions of social organisation. Even if science stand equal with classics in examinations for the services the general tenor of the public mind will in all likelihood be undisturbed. Yet it is for such a revolution that science really calls, and come it will in any community dominated by natural knowledge. Science saves us from blunders about glycerine, shows how to economise fuel and to make artificial nitrates, but these, though they decide national destinies, are merely the sheaf of the wave-offering: the harvest is behind. For natural knowledge is destined to give man not only a direct control of the material world but new interpretations of higher problems. Though we in England make a stand upon the ancient way, peoples elsewhere will move on. Those who have grasped the meaning of science, especially biological science, are feeling after new rules of conduct. The old criteria based on ignorance have little worth. "Rights," whether of persons or of nations, may be abstractions well-founded in law or philosophy, but the modern world sooner or later will annul them.

The general ignorance of science has lasted so long that we have virtually two codes of right and duty, that founded on natural truth and that emanating from tradition, which almost alone finds public expression in this country. Whether we look at the cruelty which passes for justice in our criminal courts, at the prolongation of suffering which custom demands as a part of medical ethics, at this very question of education, or indeed at any problem of social life, we see ahead and know that science proclaims wiser and gentler creeds. When in the wider sphere of national policy we read the declared ideals of statesmen, we turn away with a shrug. They bid us exalt national sentiment as a purifying and redeeming influence, and in the next breath proclaim that the sole way to avert the ruin now menacing the world is to guarantee to all nations freedom to develop, "unhindered, unthreatened, unafraid." So, forsooth, are we to end war. Nature laughs at such dreams. The life of one is the death of another. Where are the teeming populations of the West Indies, where the civilisations of Mexico or of Peru, where are the blackfellows of Australia? Since means of subsistence are limited, the fancy that one group can increase or develop save at the expense of another is an illusion, instantly dissipated by appeal to biological fact, nor would a biologist-statesman look for permanent stability in a multiplication of competing communities, some vigorous, others worthless, but all growing in population. Rather must a people familiar with science see how small and ephemeral a thing is the pride of nations, knowing that both the peace of the world and the progress of civilisation are to be sought not by the hardening of national boundaries but in the substitution of cosmopolitan for national aspiration.

VIII

ATHLETICS

By F. B. MALIM
Master of Haileybury College

At a conference held by the Froebel Society in January, 1917, the subject for discussion was the employment of women teachers in boys' schools. With some of the questions considered, whether women should have shorter hours than men, whether they are capable of enforcing discipline, and the like, I am not now concerned; but I was interested to hear from one speaker after another that a woman was at a real disadvantage in a boys' school, because she could not take part in the games. The speakers did not come from the public schools, whose devotion to athletics constitutes, we are sometimes told, a public danger, but mainly from primary and secondary day schools in London. But none the less it was assumed that a boy's games are an essential part of his education. The same assumption is made by the managers of boys' clubs and similar organisations which are endeavouring to carry on the education of boys who have left the elementary schools at the age of fourteen. In spite of the great difficulty of finding grounds to play on in the neighbourhood of great

towns, cricket and football are encouraged by any
possible means among the working lads of our industrial centres. Games are more and more being
regarded as a desirable element in the education of
the British boy, and are provided for him and organised for him by those responsible for his environment.
But this is quite a modern development. I have
been told by one who was at Marlborough in the very
early days of that school, that so far were the
authorities from providing any means of playing
cricket, that the boys themselves were obliged to
subscribe small sums for the purchase of the necessary material. The book containing the names of
the subscribers fell into the hands of the head master,
who gated for the term all boys on the list, assuming
without inquiry that they were the clients of a juvenile
bookmaker.

When we ask why we have come to regard games
as a part of a boy's education, we shall naturally
answer first that a full education is concerned with
the proper development of the body. For this purpose
we may employ the old fashioned gymnastic exercises,
the modern Swedish exercises or outdoor games. And
of these the greatest is games. "So far," says Dr
Saleeby, "as true race culture is concerned, we should
regard our muscles merely as servants or instruments
of the will. Since we have learnt to employ external
forces for our purposes, the mere bulk of a muscle is
now a matter of little importance. Of the utmost
importance, on the other hand, is the power to co-
ordinate and graduate the activity of our muscles,

so that they may become highly trained servants. This is a matter however not of muscle at all, but of nervous education. Its foundation cannot be laid by mechanical things, like dumb-bells and exercises, but by games in which will and purpose and co-ordination are incessantly employed. In other words the only physical culture worth talking about is nervous culture. The principles here laid down are daily defied in very large measure in our nurseries, our schools and our barrack yards. The play of a child, spontaneous and purposeful, is supremely human and characteristic. Although when considered from the outside, it is simply a means of muscular development, properly considered it is really the means of nervous development. Here we see muscles used as human muscles should be used, as instruments of mind. In schools the same principles should be recognised. From the biological and psychological point of view, the playing field is immensely superior to the gymnasium[1]."

It would be a mistake to under-estimate the value of the Swedish system of physical exercises. Its object is not the abnormal development of muscle, but the production of a healthy, alert and well balanced body. The military authorities in the last three years have been confronted with the problem of restoring promptness of movement, erectness of carriage, poise and flexibility to numbers of men whose muscles have been given a one-sided development by the constant performance of one kind of

---

[1] C. W. Saleeby, *Parenthood and Race Culture*, pp. 62, 63.

manual work, or have grown flabby by long sitting at a desk, and the task would have been much less successfully tackled without the aid of the Swedish methods. In schools these exercises may be used with real benefit given two conditions, small classes and a really skilled instructor. For the value a boy derives from the exercises, to a very large extent depends upon himself, on the concentration of his own will. It is almost impossible to make sure in a large class that this concentration is given, and any kind of exercise done without purpose or resolution rapidly degenerates into the most useless gesticulations. But though we may use physical exercises as an aid, I should be sorry to see them ever regarded as a substitute for games. Even supposing that they were an adequate substitute in the development of the body (which I doubt) they cannot claim to have an effect at all comparable to that of games in the development of character. Sometimes the most extravagant claims are put forward on behalf of athletics as a school of character, almost as extravagant as are the terms in which at other times the "brutal athlete" is denounced. I don't think it is found by experience that athletes cherish higher ideals or are more humble-minded than their less muscular fellows; I doubt if they become more charitable in their judgments or more liberal in their giving. We must carefully limit the claims we make, and then we shall find that we have surer grounds to go on. What virtues can we reasonably suppose to be developed by games? First I should put physical courage. It certainly requires courage to collar a fast and heavy opponent at football, to fall on the ball at the feet of a charging pack or to stand up to fast bowling on a bumpy wicket. Schoolboy opinion is rightly intolerant of a "funk," and we should not attach too small a value to this first of the manly virtues. Considering as we must the virtues which we are to develop in a nation, we realise that for the security of the nation courage in her young men is indispensable. That it has been bred in the sons of England is attested by the fields of Flanders and the beaches of Gallipoli. We shall therefore give no heed to those who decry the danger of some schoolboy games. For we shall remember that just as few things that are worth gaining can be won without toil, so there are some things which can only be won by taking risks. Few things are less attractive in a boy than the habit of playing for safety; in the old prudence is natural and perhaps admirable, in the young it is precocious and unlovely. But we need not introduce unnecessary risk by the matching of boys of unequal size and age. The practice, for example, of house games in which the boys of one house play together, without regard to size or skill, is very much inferior to an organisation of games by means of "sets," graded solely by the proficiency which boys have shown. In each set boys are matched with others whose skill approximates to their own; they are not overpowered by the strength of older boys and can get the proper enjoyment from the display of such skill as they possess.

And as we desire our games to foster the spirit

that faces danger, so we shall wish them to foster the spirit that faces hardship, the spirit of endurance. That is why I think that golf and lawn tennis are not fit school games; they are not painful enough. I am afraid we ought on the same ground to let racquets go, though for training in alertness and sheer skill, in the nice harmony of eye and hand racquets has no equal. But cricket, football, hockey, fives can all be painful enough; often victory is only to be won by a clinching of the teeth and the sternest resolve to "stick to it" in face of exhaustion. This is the merit of two forms of athletics which have been oftenest the subject of attack, rowing and running. Both of course should be carefully watched by the school doctor; for both careful training is necessary. But a sport which encourages boys to deny themselves luxuries, to scorn ease, to conquer bodily weariness by the exercise of the will, is not one which should be banished because for some the spirit has triumphed to the hurt of the flesh. In a self-indulgent age when sometimes it has seemed that the gibe of our enemies is true, that the most characteristic English word is "comfort," it is good to retain in our schools some forms of activity in which comfort is never considered at all. The Ithaca which was ἀγαθὴ κουροτρόφος, was also τρηχεῖα.

Again no boy can meet with real athletic success who has not learnt to control his temper. It is not merely that public opinion despises the man who is a bad loser; but that to lose your temper very often means to lose the game. It may be true that a Rugby forward does not develop his finest game until an opponènt's elbow has met his nose and given an extra spice to his onslaught. But in the majority of contests the man who keeps his head will win. Notably this is true in boxing, a fine instrument of education, whatever may be the objections to the prize ring. So dispassionate a scientist as Professor Hall in his monumental work on Adolescence, describes boxing as "a manly art, a superb school for quickness of eye and hand, decision, full of will and self-control. The moment this is lost, stinging punishment follows. Hence it is the surest of all cures for excessive irascibility, and has been found to have a most beneficial effect upon a peevish or unmanly disposition."

But perhaps the best lesson that a boy can learn from his games, is the lesson that he must play for his side and not for himself. He does not always learn it; the cricketer who plays for his average, the three-quarters who tries to score himself, are not unknown, though boyish opinion rightly condemns them. Popular school ethics are thoroughly sound on this point, and it is the virtue of inter-school and inter-house competitions, that in them a boy learns what it is to forget self and to think of a cause. There is a society outside himself which has its claim upon him, whose victory is his victory, whose defeat is his defeat. Whether victory comes through him or through another, is nothing so long as victory be won; later in life men may play games for their health's sake or for enjoyment, but they lose that thrill of intense patriotism, the more intense because of the smallness of the society that arouses it, with which they battled in the mud of some November day for the honour of their school or house. Small wonder that when school-fellows meet after years of separation, the memories to which they most gladly return, are the memories of hard-won victories and manfully contested defeats.

But victory must be won by fair means. There is a story (possibly without historical foundation) that a foreign visitor to Oxford said that the thing that struck him most in that great university was the fact that there were 3000 men there who would rather lose a game than win it by unfair means. It would be absurd to pretend that that spirit is universal: the commercial organisation of professional football and the development of betting have gone a long way to degrade a noble sport. But the standard of fair play in school games is high, and it is the encouragement of this spirit by cricket and football that renders them so valuable an aid in the activities of boys' clubs in artisan districts. It has been argued that the prevalence of this generous temper among our troops has been a real handicap in war; that we have too much regarded hostilities as a game in which there were certain rules to be observed, and that when we found ourselves matched against a foe whose object was to win by any means, fair or foul, the soldiers who were fettered by the scruples of honour were necessarily inferior to their unscrupulous foe. It has perhaps yet to be proved that in the long run the unchivalrous fighter always wins, and I doubt whether any of us would really prefer that even in war we should set aside the scruples of fair play. But in the arts and pursuits of peace that man is best equipped to play a noble part who realises that there are rules in the great game of life which an honourable man will respect, that there are advantages which he must not take. How often does some rather inarticulate hero, who has refused some tempting prospect or spurned some specious offer, explain his act of self-denial by the simple phrase of his boyhood, "I thought it wasn't quite playing the game." Schoolboy honour is not always a faultless thing; sometimes it means the hiding of real iniquity. But the honour of the playing field is a generous code, and to have learnt its rules is to have learnt the best that the public opinion of a boy community can teach.

The chairman of a great engineering firm recently told the Incorporated Association of Headmasters, that when he went to Oxford to get recruits for his firm, he did not look for men who had got a First in Greats, but for men who would have got a First, if they had worked. For these men had probably given a good deal of their time to rowing or games and had thereby learnt something of the art of dealing with men. The student who sticks to his books learns many lessons, but not this. To be captain of a house or of a school, and to do it well is to practise the art of governing on a small scale. A sore temptation to the schoolmaster is to interfere too much in school games. He sees obvious mistakes being made, wrong tactics being adopted, the wrong sides chosen, and he longs to interfere. He is anxious for victories, and forgets that after all victories are a very secondary business, that games are only a means, not an end, that if he does not let the boys really govern and make their mistakes, the game is failing to provide the training that it ought to give. It is undoubted that schools which are carefully coached by competent players, where the responsibility is largely taken out of the captain's hands, are more likely to win their matches. But much is lost, though the game may be won. The strong captain who goes his own way, chooses his own side, frames his own tactics and inspires the whole team with his own spirit, has had a practical training in the management of men which will stand him in good stead in the greater affairs of life. "We are not very well satisfied" said a War Office official, "with the stamp of young officer we are getting. Many of them never seem to have played a game in their lives, though they are first-rate mathematicians." And there is no doubt that whether for war or peace mathematics is not a substitute for leadership.

Courage, endurance, self-control, public spirit, fair play, leadership, these are the virtues which we find may be encouraged by the practice of games at school. It is not a complete list of the Christian virtues, perhaps rather we might call them Pagan virtues, but it is a fine list for all that. And the best of it is that they are as it were unconsciously learnt, acquired by practice, not by inculcation. The boy who follows virtue for its own sake would be, I fear, a sad prig, but the boy who follows a football for the sake of his house, may develop virtue and enjoy the process.

But what are we to put on the other side of the account? If it be true that athletics is a fine school for character, what is the ground for the frequent complaint that the public schools make a "fetish" of athleticism? What precisely is the complaint? It is this, that boys regard, and are encouraged to regard their games as the most important side of their school life, that their interest in them is so overpowering that they have no interest left for the development of the intellect or the acquisition of knowledge, that prominent athletes, not brilliant scholars, are the heroes of a boy community, and that in consequence many men of the better nourished classes, after they have left school, look upon their amusements as the main business of life, give to them the industry and concentration which should be bestowed upon science, letters or industry, and swell the ranks of the amiable and incompetent amateur. It is argued that schools are converted into pleasant athletic clubs, and that boys, instead of learning there to work, merely learn to play. Now this is a serious indictment; it is a good thing to learn to play, but it is not the only thing a school should teach. Riding, shooting and speaking the truth may have been an adequate curriculum for an ancient Persian, but it would not provide a sufficient equipment to enable a man to face the stress of modern competition, or to understand the developments of the science and industry of to-day.

Is too much time given to the playing of games? In winter time I should say No. I suppose that if we include teaching hours and preparation, a boy spends some six hours a day on his intellectual work, or if you prefer, he is supposed to spend that time. A game of football two or three times a week, does not last more than an hour and a quarter; if you add a liberal allowance for changing and baths, two hours is the whole time occupied. A game of fives or a physical drill class need not demand more than an hour. The game that really wastes time—and I am sorry to admit it—is cricket. I am not thinking so much of the long waits in the pavilion when two batsmen on a side are well set, and the rest have nothing to do but to applaud. I see no way out of that difficulty, so long as wickets are prepared as they are now by artistic groundsmen. I am thinking rather of the excessive practice at nets. An enthusiastic house captain is apt to believe that by assiduous practice the most unlikely and awkward recruit can be converted into a useful batsman, and the result is that he will drive all his house day after day to the nets, until they begin to loathe the sight of a cricket ball.

We should recognise that cricket is a game for the few; the majority of boys can never make good cricketers. And happy are those schools which are near a river and can provide an alternative exercise in the summer, which does not require exceptional quickness of eye and wrist and does provide a splendid discipline of body and spirit. In the summer it is well to exempt all boys from cricket, who have really a taste for natural history or photography. Summer half-holidays are emphatically the time for hobbies, and it is a serious charge against our games if they are organised to such a pitch that hobbies are practically prohibited. The zealous captain will object that such "slacking" is destroying the spirit of the house. We must endeavour to point out to him that the unwilling player never makes a good player, and that such a boy may be finding his proper development in the pursuit of butterflies, a development which he would never gain by unsuccessful and involuntary cricket. House masters too are apt to complain that freedom for hobbies is subversive of discipline, and to quote the old adage about Satan and idle hands. That there is risk, is not to be denied. But you cannot run a school without taking risks. Our whole system of leaving the government largely in the hands of boys is full of risks. Sometimes it brings shipwreck; more often it does not. For in the majority of cases the policy of confidence is justified by results.

There is one way of wasting time that is heartily to be condemned, the waste involved in looking on. I am inclined to think that if all athletic contests took place without a ring of spectators, we should get all the good of games and very little of the evil. Certainly professional football would lose its blacker sides if there were no gate money and no betting. Few men or boys are the worse for playing games; it is the applause of the mob that turns their heads. But I am afraid I am not logical enough to say that I would forbid boys to watch matches against another school; the emotions that lead to the "breathless hush in the Close" are so compounded of patriotism and jealousy for the honour of the school, that they are far from ignoble. But I would not have boys compelled to watch the games against clubs and other non-school teams. Above all, if they watch, they must have a run or a game to stir their own blood. The half-holiday must not be spent in shivering on a touchline and then crowding round a fire.

That the athlete is a school hero and the scholar is not, is most certainly true. The scholar may once in a way reflect glory on the school by success in an examination, but generally he is regarded as a self-regarding person, who is not likely to help to win the matches of the year. But the hero-worship is not undiscriminating; conceit, selfishness, surliness will go far to nullify the influence of physical strength and skill. Boys' admiration for physical prowess is natural and not unhealthy. The harm is done by the advertisement given to such prowess by foolish elders. Foremost among such unwise influences I should put the press. Even modest boys may begin to think their achievements in the field are of public importance when they find their names in print. Some papers publish portraits of prominent players, or a series of articles on "Football at X—" or "The prospects of the Cricket Season at Y—". The suggestion that there is a public which is interested in the features of a schoolboy captain, or wishes to know the methods of training and coaching which have led to the success of a school fifteen, is likely to give boys an entirely exaggerated notion of their own importance and to justify in their minds the dedication of a great deal of time to the successes which receive this kind of public recognition.

Next there is the parent. Our ever active critics are apt to forget that schools are to a large extent mirrors, reflecting the tone and opinion of the homes from which boys come. The parent who says when the boy joins the school, "I do not mind whether he gets in the sixth, but I want to see him in the eleven," is by no means an uncommon parent. I have no objection to his wanting to see his boy in the eleven, the deplorable thing is that he is indifferent to intellectual progress. I have heard an elder brother say, "Tom has not got into his house eleven yet, but he brought home a prize last term. I have written to tell him he must change all that, we can't have him disgracing the family." When a candidate has failed to qualify for admission to the school at the entrance examination, I have had letters of surprised and pained protest, pointing out that Jack is an exceptionally promising cricketer. It is assumed that we should be only too glad to welcome the athlete without regard to his standard of work. If we could get the majority of parents to recognise the school-master's point of view, that while games are an important element of education, they are only one element, and that there are others which must not be neglected, we should have made a real step forward towards the elimination of the excessive reverence paid to the athlete.

After the press and the parent comes millinery. Perhaps it is Utopian to suggest that "caps" can be entirely, abolished; but the enterprise of haberdashers and the weakness of school authorities have led to a multiplication of blazers, ribbons, caps, jerseys, stockings, badges, scarves and the like, which certainly tend to mark off the successful player from his fellows, and to make him a cynosure of the vulgar and an object of complacent admiration to himself. Success in games should be its own reward. In some cases it certainly is. And the paradox is that very often it is those who are least bountifully endowed by nature who profit most. Some there are who have such natural gifts of strength and dexterity, that from the first they can excel at any game. Triumphs come to them without hard struggle, and they breathe the incense of applause. But others have a clumsier hand, a slower foot, and yet they have a determination to excel, a resolution in sticking to their task that brings them at the last to a fair measure of skill. Such a boy is already rewarded by the toughening of the will that perseverance brings: he does not need a ribbon on his sweater. To give the other, the natural athlete, a coloured scarf, is to run the risk of making him over-value the gifts he owes to nature.

There is no reason why a boy who excels in games should not excel in work. The two are not competing sides of education, they are complementary. The schoolmaster's ideal is that his boys should gain the advantages of both. The athlete who neglects his work, grows up with a poorly furnished mind and an untrained judgment. The student who neglects his games, grows up without the nervous development that fits his body to be the instrument of his will, and without the knowledge of men and the habit of dealing with men which are indispensable in many callings. It has been proved again and again that it is possible to get the advantages of both these sides of school life. There is no reason why the playing of school games should be anything but a help to the intellectual development of a boy.

But the constant talking about games is by no means harmless, though it is true boys might be talking of worse things. It is related that a French educational critic was once descanting to an English head master on the monotony of the conversation of English public school boys: "they talk of nothing but football." But when he was asked, "And of what do French school boys generally talk?" he was silent. But if "cricket shop" saves us from worse topics, it certainly is destructive of rational conversation on subjects of more general interest. In great boarding schools we collect a population of boys under quite abnormal conditions, cut off for the greater part of their social life from intercourse with older people. It is, I think, a general experience that boys who have been at day schools and are the sons of intelligent parents, have their minds more awakened to the questions of the day in politics, or art, or literature than boys of equal ability who have been at a boarding school. They have had the advantage of hearing their father and his friends discussing topics which are outside the range of school life. Boarding schools are often built in some country place away from the surging life of towns, where the noise of political strife and the roar of the traffic of the world are but dimly heard. In such seclusion the life of the school, particularly the active life of the playing fields, occupies the focus of a boy's consciousness. The geographical conditions tend to narrow the range of his interests, and he remains a boy when others are growing to be men. Those who have the wider tastes, are deterred from talking about them by the ever present fear of "side." They will talk freely to a master of architecture or music or Japanese prints, but they are chary of betraying these enthusiasms to their fellows. And masters are not free from blame: I suppose we all of us sometimes bow down in the house of Rimmon, and when the conversation languishes at the tea-table, fall back on a discussion of the last house match. It is the line of least resistance, and after a strenuous day's work it is not easy to maintain a monologue about Home Rule. Not the least of the boons of the war is that it has ousted games from the foremost place as a topic of conversation. I have not noticed that they are less keenly played, although the increase of military work has diminished the time given to them; but they have ceased to monopolise the thoughts of boys. The problem then of reducing the absorption in games is the problem of finding and providing other absorbing interests.

We cannot, fortunately, always have the counter-irritant of war. Where we fail now, is that the intellectual training of a boy does not interest him enough in most cases to give him subjects of conversation out of school. We give some few new interests by means of societies, literary, antiquarian or scientific. But the main problem is to make every boy see that the work he does in school is connected with his life, that it is meant to open to him the shut doors around him through which he may go out into all the highways and byways of the world.

Do school games produce the man who regards games as the main business of life? We must emphasise "main." It is certain that they do encourage Englishmen to devote some part of their working life to healthy exercise—and few, I suppose, would wish them to do otherwise. The Indian civilian does not make a worse judge for playing polo, nor is Benin worse administered since golf-links were laid out there. But there are men who never outgrow the boyish narrowness of view that games are the things that matter most. These remain the ruling passion, because no stronger passion comes to drive it out. For this the schools must bear part of the blame, for they have not taught clearly enough that athletics are a means but not an end. Not all the blame, for surely some must rest on a society which tolerates the idler, and has no reproach for the man who says "I live only for hunting and golf." And here as elsewhere, I believe we are judged more by a few failures than by many successes. We can all of us in our experience recall many an honest athlete who is now doing splendid service to Church or State, doughty curates, self-sacrificing doctors, soldiers who are real leaders of men. When they became men they put away childish things, but they have not forgotten what they owe to the discipline of their boyish games. Games are not the first thing in life for them now, but they have no doubt that they can do their work better from an occasional afternoon's play. They see things in their right proportion, because they know that the first thing is to have a job and do it well. If we can teach boys to begin to understand that truth while they are at school, we shall have exorcised the bogey of athleticism. I should expect to find (though I do not know) that the authorities at Osborne and Dartmouth do not need to bother their minds about that bogey. Their boys play games with all a sailor's heartiness, but their ambition is not to be a first-class athlete, but to be a first-class sailor, and the games take their proper place. It may be desirable to reduce the time devoted to games, though as I have said I doubt if there is any need to do so, except for cricket. It may be that we should give more time to handicraft, or military drill. But these things will not change the spirit. What we need to do is to make clearer the object of education in which athletics form a part, that there may be more sense of reality in the boy's school time, more understanding that he is at school to fit himself manfully and capably to play his part on the wider stage of life.

IX

THE USE OF LEISURE

By J. H. BADLEY

Head Master of Bedales School

To teach a sensible use of leisure, healthy both for mind and body, is by no means the least important part of education. Nor is it by any means the least pressing, or the least difficult, of school problems. "Loafing" at times that have no recognised duties assigned them, is generally a sign of slackness in work and play as well; and if we do not find occupation for thoughts and hands, the rhyme tells us who will. The devils of cruelty and uncleanness will be ready to enter the empty house, and fill it at least with unwholesome talk, and thoughtless if not ill-natured "ragging." Yet work and games, whatever keenness we arouse and encourage in these, cannot fill a boy's whole time and thoughts—or, if they do, his life, whether he is student or athlete, or even the occasional combination of both, is still a narrow one and likely to get narrower as years go by. If life to the un-educated means a soulless round of labour varied by the public-house and the "pictures," so to the half-educated it is apt, except in war time, to mean the office and the club, with interests that do not go beyond golf and motoring and bridge. If our lives are emptier and our interests narrower than they need be, it is partly the result of a narrow and unsatisfying education, which leaves half our powers undeveloped and interests untouched, and too often only succeeds in giving us a distaste for those which it touches. Both for the sake of the present, therefore, to avoid the dangers of unfilled leisure, and still more for the sake of the future, the wise schoolmaster does all he can to foster, in addition to keenness in the regular work and games, interests, both individual and social, of other kinds as well. He will make opportunities for various handicrafts: he will try to stimulate lines of investigation not arranged for in the class-routine; he will encourage the formation of societies both for discussion and active pursuits, for instruction and entertainment. It is the purpose of this essay to suggest what, along these lines, is possible in the school.

But the reasons so far given for the encouragement of leisure-time interests are mainly negative. In order to realise to the full the importance of this side of education, we must look rather at their positive value. From whichever point of view one looks at it, physical, intellectual, or social, this value is not small. Some of these interests contribute directly to health in being outdoor pursuits; and these, in not letting games furnish the only motive and means of exercise, can help to establish habits and motives of no little help in later life, when games are no longer easy to keep up. And even in the years when the call of games is strongest, some rivalry of other outdoor

pursuits is useful as a preventive of absorption in
athleticism, easily carried to excess at school so as to
shut out finer interests and influences.   It was a consciousness of this that led Captain Scott, in the letter
written in those last hours among the Antarctic snows,
thinking of his boy at home, and the education that
he wished for him, to write: "Make the boy interested
in natural history, if you can; it is better than games:
they encourage it in some schools."

Besides health—and health, we must remember,
is not only a bodily matter, but depends on mental
as well as bodily activity, and on the enjoyment of
the activity that comes from its being mainly voluntary
—the pursuits that we are considering can do much
to train skill of various kinds.   The class-work represents the minimum that we expect a boy to know;
but there is much that necessarily lies outside it of
hardly less value.   Many a boy learns as much from
the hobby on which he spends his free time as from
the work he does in class.   Sometimes, indeed, such
a free-time hobby reveals the bent that might otherwise have gone undiscovered, and determines the
choice of a special line of work for the future career.

But the chief value of such interests lies rather in
their influence on other work, and on the general
development of character.   In giving scope for many
kinds of skill, they are helping the intellectual training;
and however ready we may be to pay lip-service to
the principle of learning by doing, and to admit the
educational importance of the hand in brain-develop-
ment, in most of our school work we still ignore these

things, so far as any practical application of them is concerned. One is sometimes tempted to wonder if in the future there may not be so complete a reaction from our present ideas and methods as to make what are now regarded as mere hobbies the main matter of education, and to relegate much of the present school course, as the writing of verses has already been relegated, to the category of optional side-shows. At any rate these free-time interests can supply a very useful stimulus to much of the routine work. In these a boy may find himself for the first time, and discover, despite his experience in class, that he is no fool. Or at least he may find there a centre of interest, otherwise lacking, round which other interests can group, and to which knowledge obtained in various class-subjects can attach itself, and so get for him a meaning and a use. And further, if we do not make the mistake of narrowing the range of choice, and allow, at any rate at first, a succession of interests, the very range and variety of these pursuits is an antidote against the tendency to early specialisation, encouraged by scholarship and entrance examinations, which is one of the dangers against which we need to be on our guard. If, therefore, without mere dissipation of interest, we can widen the range of mental activities and encourage, by discussions, essays, lectures and so forth, reading round and outside the subjects dealt with in class, this is all to the good.

And all this has a social as well as an individual aspect. The meetings for the purposes just mentioned, as well as those for entertainment, have, like games, a real educational value, and do much to cement the comradeship of common interests and common aims that is one of the best things school has to give. And not only among those of the same age. These are things in which the example and influence of the older are particularly helpful to the younger. They can become, like the games, and perhaps to an even greater extent, one of the interests that help to bind together past and present members of a school. And they afford an opportunity for masters to meet boys on a more personal and friendly footing, and to get the mutual knowledge and respect which are all-important if education is to be, in Thring's definition, a transmission of life through the living to the living. That the organisation of leisure-time pursuits is of the utmost help to the school as well as to the boy, is the unanimous verdict of the schools in which it has long been a tradition. The master who has had charge, for the past five-and-twenty years, of this organisation in one such school writes that there they consider such pursuits as the very life-blood of the school, and the only rational method of maintaining discipline.

If what has here been said is admitted, it is plain that to teach, by every means in our power, the use of leisure, is one of the most important things a school has to do. We might, therefore, turn at once to the consideration of the various means for such teaching that experience has shown to be practicable in the school. But before doing so, there is yet another reason, the most far-reaching of all, to be urged for regarding this as a side of education fully as necessary, at the present time above all, as those sides that none would question. Great as is the direct and immediate value of the interests and occupations thus to be encouraged, their indirect influence is more valuable still, if they teach not only handiness and adaptiveness, but also call forth initiative and individuality, and so help to develop the complete and many-sided human personality which is the crown and purpose of education as of life. We do not now think of education as merely book-learning, nor even as concerned only with mind and body, or only as fitting preparation for skilled work and cultured leisure; but rather as the development of the whole human being, with all his possibilities, interests, and motives, as well as powers, his feelings and imagination no less than reason and will. In a word, education is training for life, with all that this connotes, and, as we learn to live only by living, must be thought of not merely as preparation for life, but as a life itself. Plainly, if we give it a meaning as wide as this, a great part of education lies outside the school, in the influences of the home surroundings and, after school, of occupation and the whole social environment. But during the school years—and they are the most impressionable of all— it is the school life that is for most the chief formative influence; and now more necessarily so than ever. When, a few generations back, life was still, in the main, life in the country, and most things were still made at home or in the village, the most important part of education lay, except for a few, outside the school. Now it is the other way. Town life, the

replacing of home-made by factory-made goods, the
disappearance of the best part of home life before the
demands of industry on the one side and the growth
of luxury on the other—these things are signs of a
tendency that has swept away most of the practical
home-education, and thrown it all upon the school.
And the schools have even yet hardly realised the
full meaning of this change. Instead of having to
provide only a part of education—the specially intellectual and, in the public schools at least, the
physical side—we have now to think of the whole
nature of the growing boy or girl, and, by the environment and the occupations we provide, to appeal
to interests and motives, and give occasion for the
right use of powers, that may otherwise be undeveloped
or misused. A school cannot now consist merely of
class-rooms and playing fields. This is recognised by
the addition of laboratories and workshops, gymnasium, swimming-bath, lecture-hall, museum, art-
school, music-rooms—all now essentials of a day school
as much as of a boarding school. But many of
these things are still only partially made use of, and
are apt to be regarded rather as ornamental ex-
crescences, to be used by the few who have a special
bent that way, at an extra charge, than as an integral
part of education for all. All the interests and means
of training that they represent, and others as well,
need to be brought more into the daily routine; to
some extent in place of the too exclusively literary,
or at least bookish, training, that has hitherto been
the staple of education, but more, perhaps, since it is

not possible to include in the regular curriculum *all* that is of value, as optional subjects and free-time occupations, though organised as part of the school course. For it is not only the few who already know their bent who need opportunity to be made for following it, but rather those who will not discover their powers without practice, or their interests without suggestion or encouragement. In this respect the war has brought opportunities of no little value to the school, not only in the absorbing interest in the war itself and the desire for knowledge and readiness for effort that it awakens, but also in the demands it has made for practical work of many kinds that boys and girls can do, and the lessons of service that it has taught. Work on the land and in the shops, for those whose school time is already too short, is a curtailment, only to be made as a last resort, of the kind of learning they will have no other opportunity to acquire; but it gives to the public school boy the feeling of reality that most of his school work lacks. Such opportunities of doing what is seen to be productive and necessary work, are, like the making of things for those at the front, and for the wounded, both in themselves and in the motives that inspire them, a valuable part of education that should not be forgotten when the present need for them is over.

If, then, by the fullest use of leisure occupations, we are, like Canning, to call in a new world to redress the balance of the old, what, in actual practice, is possible in the school? For an answer to this question one has only to see what is done in the schools of the

Society of Friends, in which the use of leisure in these ways has always been a strongly marked feature long before it was taken up by others, with a tradition, indeed, in the older schools, of sixty or a hundred years of accumulated experience behind it. Instead of singling out, for description of the use it makes of leisure, any one school in which it might be supposed that there were special conditions present, it will be best to enumerate the various activities that have long been practised in several different schools. Of those selected for the purpose not all are connected with the Society of Friends; some are for boys and some for girls only, and some co-educational; but alike in being boarding schools, and in keeping their boys and girls from an early age until, at the end of their school life, they go on to the university or to their business or professional training. A few of the pursuits to be mentioned are obviously more appropriate for boys, others for girls; but the differences between those that are followed in schools for boys and those for girls are surprisingly small, and to give separate lists would only involve much needless repetition.

For the sake of clearness, it may be well to group the various activities according as they are mainly outdoor or indoor occupations. In the outdoor group, games and sports need not be included, as being, in most cases, as much a part of the ordinary school course as the class-work. They only become free-time pursuits, in the sense here intended, in so far as practice for them is optional, and a large amount of free time spent upon it. Thus, for example, while swimming is, or should be, compulsory for all, and a regular time found for it in the school time-table, it is entirely a voluntary matter to go in, as in many schools a large number do, for the tests of the Royal Humane Society. Apart from games, the outdoor pursuit that occupies the largest place is probably, in most of these schools, some branch of natural history (which may perhaps be held to include geology as well as the study of plant and animal life)—not so much by the making of collections, though this usually serves as a beginning, as by the keeping of diaries, notes of observations illustrated by drawings and photographs, and experimental work, in connection, perhaps, with work done in science classes. Similarly in the study of archaeology, visits to places of interest —there are always many old churches within reach, if not other buildings of equal interest—give matter for written notes as well as for drawings and photographs; and in at least one case, the fact that the neighbourhood is rich in Roman remains has given opportunity, under the guidance of a keen classical archaeologist, for the laying bare of more than one Roman villa, and for making interesting additions to the school museum. Besides their use in the service of other pursuits, sketching and photography also have many votaries for their own sake, though the former is usually more dependent on encouragement from above. Then there is gardening. The tenure of a plot of ground is a joy to many children; and in the opinion of the writer, some experience, and some experimental work, in the growing of the most necessary food plants, as well as flowers, should form part of the education of all at a certain stage, whether in school time or in free time. For some, where the conditions are favourable, this can be extended to the care of fruit-trees, bees, poultry, and to some kinds of farm-work. The needs of war-time have brought something of this into many schools, to the real gain of education, now and later, if it can be retained, at least as a possibility of choice. So also with the care of the playing fields: the more that the work needed for a game is thrown upon the players themselves, the more does it contribute to education. And so too with constructive work of any kind that, with some help of suggestion or direction, is within the compass even of comparatively unskilled labour. A lengthy list could be given of things accomplished in this way, with an educational value all the greater for their practical purpose, from Ruskin's famous road down to the last field levelled and pavilion built or shed put up, by voluntary effort and in time found by the workers without encroaching on regular school work. And lastly, an outdoor occupation for free time which, in the earlier days of school life, we shall do well to encourage—both for its own value and the manifold interests that it encourages and lessons that it teaches, and also for its bearing on questions of national service that will remain to be answered after the war—is the wide range of activities comprised in scouting, undoubtedly one of the chief educational advances of our time. Whatever differences of views there may be on the wider questions of military service for national defence, and of making military training a specific part of education, few can deny that, with a view to national service of *some* kind, the use made by Sir Robert Baden-Powell of instincts natural to all at a particular stage of growth, by an organisation which can be kept entirely free from the failings of militarism, is a development of the utmost educational, as well as national, value. If a school already develops, by other means, all the activities trained by scouting, and utilises in other ways the instincts and motives to which it makes appeal, there may be little or nothing to be gained by its adoption. But of how many schools can this be said? For the rest it undoubtedly offers a way of doing, at the stage of growth for which it is best fitted, much of what, if there is any truth in what has been urged above, is, from the point of view of individual development, of greater importance now than ever before. If, in addition to this, it will go far to solve the problem of national service, and to remove the need for conscription in the continental form, there is every reason to give it a prominent place in the activities encouraged, if not insisted upon, at school.

Let us now turn to the group of indoor pursuits, which, if they have not quite so direct a bearing upon health, are in another way even more important; for a large part of leisure, even at school and still more, in all probability, afterwards, falls at times and under conditions that make some indoor occupation necessary, and the waste or misuse of these times is likely to be greater. In this group certain things need be no more than mentioned, as either applying, at any given time, only to a few picked individuals, or else likely, in the majority of schools, to be made a regular part of the school routine; such as, of the one kind, the editing of the school magazine, or membership of the school fire-brigade with the frequent practices that this involves; or, of the other kind, special gymnastics (including such things as boxing and fencing), or lectures and concerts and other entertainments given to the school, as distinguished from those given by members of it, the preparation for which gives occupation beforehand to much of their leisure. Of the free-time pursuits more properly so called, in which many can share, the commonest are probably the various school societies. Most schools have one or more debating societies, with meetings at regular intervals throughout the winter terms, for the discussion of questions of general or special interest; the difficulty being more often to find a subject than speakers. Many also have Essay or Literary societies, for reading papers and discussing the books and writers treated of, which involve a considerable amount of previous reading. Besides these most schools now have similar societies, in addition to those for carrying out the field-work already mentioned, for holding lectures and discussions on various branches of science. Some also have a musical society for gaining fuller acquaintance with the works of the chief composers; and a dramatic society for reading and acting plays as occasion allows. Allied with these interests is voluntary laboratory work in some branch of science, both by individuals and groups, which may not unfairly be dignified with the name of research, even if it is only the re-discovery of what has been worked out by others. In some schools special provision is made for encouraging optional work of this kind in astronomy; in others it may be wireless telegraphy, or the use of vegetable dyes, and so forth. In some of this work even the younger can take part; and of the many reasons for its encouragement not the least is the wide field it opens to individual initiative.

Besides all these more specially intellectual interests, and of still wider appeal, various kinds of handicrafts afford abundant occupation, some for the longer and some also for the shorter periods of leisure. Wood-work, carving, work in metal or leather, pottery, basket-plaiting, bookbinding, needlework and embroidery, knitting, netting hammocks and so forth— the only limit to the number of such crafts is the limit to the knowledge and energy of those who can start and direct them, and to the space available, as some can only be carried on in rooms reserved for such work. So, too, with various kinds of art-work— drawing, modelling, lettering, making posters for entertainments; or music, both individual and concerted, orchestra practice, part-singing, glee-clubs and so on; or morrice and other folk-dances, now happily being widely revived. And lastly there are indoor games, some of which, like chess (cards are probably best confined to the sanatorium), have a high training value, and others afford a useful occasional outlet to high spirits; and entertainments got up by some society, or perhaps by a single form, for the rest of the "house" or school, such as a concert or play or even an occasional fancy-dress dance, the preparation for which will happily occupy free time for as long beforehand as is allowed, and does much to encourage ingenuity, especially if strict conditions are imposed that all that is required must be made for the purpose and not bought.

But by this time many questions will have arisen in the mind of the reader, especially if much of what has been enumerated lies outside his school experience; questions that demand an immediate answer. Even if all this free-time work and play may have a certain value, how can time be found for it without encroaching on the regular work and games which, after all, must be the main concern of the school? And even supposing that time could be found for both, will not all this voluntary activity and pleasure-work absorb the interests and energies that ought to be given to the more serious, if less attractive, studies? And again, how can all this wide range of activity be controlled? Who is going to teach, or look after, all these things? How are they to be kept going? Are they, or any of them, to be compulsory, or is a boy or girl to be allowed to do anything or nothing, or to flit, butterfly-fashion, from one to another, learning nothing except to fritter away energy in endless mental dissipation?

Only a brief answer can be attempted to these questions. It might indeed be given in the answer to the old puzzle, *solvitur ambulando*; for, given a

clear aim and common sense, most difficulties in education disappear as one goes on. It is, in fact, a
question of educational values; that settled, matters
of detail soon settle themselves. From what has been
said above, it will be plain that the writer is one of
those who think these voluntary free-time activities of
such value that they are willing, in order to make room
for them, to jettison some of the traditions that
have gathered about school work and games. Let the
morning hours be reserved for the severer kinds of
class work, but let the afternoons be mainly given to
active pursuits of other kinds as well as games; and
on one of them at least let expeditions in pursuit of
the outdoor interests above outlined be an alternative
to the games chosen by the keen players, or compulsory for those without an equivalent hobby. Then,
too, in the evenings let preparation be varied with
handicrafts (the result will be an intellectual gain
rather than loss), and time be reserved for the meetings
of societies or for entertainments. It may be well to
say here that while every one of the things above
mentioned is an actual fact in some school, in none,
probably, are all attempted at once, nor, of course, do
any of their members take up many of these pursuits
at the same time; but it is surprising how much can
be done by treating a part of some afternoons and
evenings in the week as leisure time for these pursuits.
When this is done, there is usually a particular member
of the Staff whose task it is, either permanently or in
rotation, to see what is being done, to give suggestions
and encouragement to beginners, and to see, if

necessary, that freedom does not mean disorder. Naturally, in the case of handicrafts, others also take part as actual teachers or at least as fellow-workers; but though it is generally helpful for members of the Staff to join in all such work and in discussions, the aim of it all is likely to be more fully attained if as much as possible of the organisation and direction is left to members of the school. So, too, with the question of compulsion. Not all have so strong a bent as to know what they want to do, and sometimes interests come only by actual experience. It is well, therefore, to have an understanding that, at certain times, all must follow some one of the possible occupations; but the more it can be left to the individual choice, and the wider the range of choice, the better for the purpose we have in view. Not all country rambles need have a definite object, nor all time be actively filled that might be left for reading. But without a definite object few will make a habit of walking, or learn to know and love the country; and not all, especially where there is a multiplicity of other interests, will form the habit of reading unless regular times are set apart for it, times when books must be read and not merely magazines. How far freedom of change from one occupation to another is desirable is largely an individual question. The younger need to try many things before they can settle down to one, in order to discover their real interests and to exercise their faculties. But it is well to have a strict limit to the number of things that may be taken up at once, and a fixed length of time to be given to each before it may be replaced by another. With the older, this, as a rule, settles itself, on the one hand by growing interest in one or two directions, and on the other by the increasing demands of the school work and approaching examinations. It is the younger, therefore, who need most encouragement. In schools where, as said above, there is a long tradition of such free-time work, there is the less need for anything beyond suggestions and general supervision. Yet even in these it is found helpful to have, at the beginning of the year, talks upon the subject by some member of the Staff, or an old boy perhaps who has devoted himself to some particular branch, in order to explain what can be done and the standard to be maintained. In several of them prizes are offered every year, either by the school or by the Old Scholars' Association or by individual old scholars, for good work in many of the categories mentioned above; these in some schools being the only prizes given. In some cases they are money prizes, as in certain kinds of work the tools or materials used are costly; in others the prizes are not given to individuals, but in the form of a "trophy" to the form or "house" that shows up the best record for the term or year; in others, again, the need of prizes is not felt, but interest and keenness to maintain a good standard are kept up by the public show, held each year, of work done in leisure time. And, it may be added, a great stimulus in itself is the wider freedom that can be earned by those who follow certain branches of study, in the way, for instance, of expeditions, on foot or by bicycle, to places where they can be pursued.

But with all this there is, of course, the danger that so much energy may be absorbed in these pursuits that little is left for the ordinary school work. In some few cases, where there is a strong natural bent and the free-time pursuit is a serious object of study, this may be a thing not to be discouraged, as it will provide the truest means of education. But in most cases care is needed to see that the due proportion is kept, and especially that mere amusement is not allowed to occupy the whole of leisure, still less to distract thought and effort from serious work. By making entertainments, which might, if too frequent or too elaborate, have this effect, dependent on the school work being well done, this danger can be minimised. For the rest, if free-time work is found to take the first place in a boy's thoughts, may not this be a sign that the ordinary curriculum and methods of teaching are capable of improvement, and that more use of these natural interests may with advantage be made in class time as well? Not that work of any kind can be all pleasure or always outwardly interesting; there is plenty of hard spade-work needed in any study seriously followed, in class or out. But if in education keenness is the first essential and personality the final aim, interest and freedom must have a larger place than is usually allowed them in the class-room if the real education is not to centre in the self-chosen and self-directed pursuits of leisure.

One word more. It must not be supposed that all that has been described is only possible, or only needed, in the boarding school or only for a specially leisured class. If, as has here been urged, these activities and interests form an integral part of education in its fullest meaning, they are just as necessary in the day school and cannot be left to chance and the home to see to. And of all the needed reforms in elementary education, amongst the most needed is the greater utilisation of the active interests and instincts of children, in a training that would have a wider outlook and a closer bearing, through practical experience, both on the work of life and the use of leisure.

X

PREPARATION FOR PRACTICAL LIFE

By SIR J. D. McCLURE
Head Master of Mill Hill School

I

It is, perhaps, the chief glory of the Ideal Commonwealth that each and every member thereof is found in his right place. His profession is also his vocation; in it is his pride; through it he attains to the *joie de vivre*; by it he makes his contribution to the happiness of his fellows and to the welfare and progress of the State. The contemplation of the Ideal, however, would seem to be nature's anodyne for experience of the Actual. In practical life, all attempts, however earnest and continuous, to realise this ideal are frustrated by one or more of many difficulties; and though the Millennium follows hard upon Armageddon, we cannot assume that in the period vaguely known as "after the war" these difficulties will be fewer in number or less in magnitude. Some of the more obvious may be briefly considered.

In theory, every child is "good for something"; in practice, all efforts to discover for what some children are good prove unavailing. The napkin may be shaken never so vigorously, but the talent remains hidden. In every school there are many honest fellows who seem to have no decided bent in any direction, and who would probably do equally well, or equally badly, in any one of half-a-dozen different employments. Some of these boys are steady, reliable, not unduly averse from labour, willing—even anxious— to be guided and to carry out instructions, yet are quite unable to manifest a preference for any one kind of work.

Others, again, show real enthusiasm for a business or profession, but do not possess those qualities which are essential to success therein; yet they are allowed to follow their supposed bent, and spend the priceless years of adolescence in the achievement of costly failure. Many a promising mechanic has been spoiled by the ill-considered attempts to make a passable engineer; and the annals of every profession abound in parallel instances of misdirected zeal. In saying this, however, one would not wish to undervalue enthusiasm, nor to deny that it sometimes reveals or develops latent and unsuspected talents.

The life-work of many is determined largely, if not entirely, by what may be termed family considerations. There is room for a boy in the business of his father or some other relative. The fitness of the boy for the particular employment is not, as a rule, seriously considered; it is held, perhaps, to be sufficiently proved by the fact that he is his father's son. He is more likely to be called upon to recognise the special dispensations of a beneficent Providence on his behalf.

It is natural that a man should wish the fruits of his labour to benefit his family in the first instance, at any rate; and the desire to set his children well on the road of life's journey seems entirely laudable. It is easy to hold what others have won, to build on foundations which others have laid, and to do this with all their experience and goodwill to aid him. Hence when the father retires he has the solid satisfaction of knowing that

> Resigned unto the Heavenly Will,
> His son keeps on the business still.

It cannot be denied that this policy is often successful; but it is equally undeniable that it is directly responsible for the presence of many incompetent men in positions which none but the most competent should occupy. There are many long-established firms hastening to decay because even they are not strong enough to withstand the disastrous consequences of successive infusions of new (and young) blood.

Many, too, are deterred from undertaking congenial work by reason of the inadequate income to be derived therefrom, and the unsatisfactory prospects which it presents. Let it suffice to mention the teaching profession, which fails to attract in any considerable numbers the right kind of men and women. A large proportion of its members did not become teachers from deliberate choice, but, having failed in their attempt to secure other employment, were forced to betake themselves to the ever-open portals of the great Refuge for the Destitute, and become teachers (or, at least, become classified as such). True there are a few "prizes" in the profession, and to some of the *rude donati* the Church holds out a helping hand; but the lay members cannot look forward even to the "congenial gloom of a Colonial Bishopric."

Others, again, are attracted to employments (for which they may have no special aptitude) by the large salaries or profits which are to be earned therein, often with but little trouble or previous training—or so, at least, they believe. The idea of vocation is quite obscured, and a man's occupation is in effect the shortest distance from poverty which he cannot endure, to wealth and leisure which he may not know how to use.

It frequently happens, too, that a young man is unable to afford either the time or the expense necessary to qualify for the profession which he desires to enter, and for which he is well adapted by his talents and temperament. Not a few prefer in such circumstances to "play for safety," and secure a post in the Civil Service.

It is plain from such considerations as these that all attempts to realise the Utopian ideal must needs be, for the present at least, but very partially successful. Politics are not the only sphere in which "action is one long second-best." Even if it were possible at the present time to train each youth for that calling which his own gifts and temperament, or the reasoned judgment of his parents, selected as his life-work, it is very far from certain that he would ultimately find himself engaged therein. English institutions are largely based on the doctrine of

individual liberty, and those statutes which establish
or safeguard individual rights are not unjustly regarded as the "bulwarks of the Constitution." But
the inalienable right of a father to choose a profession
for his son, or of the son to choose one for himself, is
often exercised without any real inquiry into the conditions of success in the profession selected. Hence
the frequent complaints about the "overcrowding of
the professions" either in certain localities or in the
country at large. The Bar affords a glaring example.
"There be many which are bred unto the law, yet is
the law not bread unto them." The number of recruits
which any one branch of industry requires in a single
year is not constant, and, in some cases, is subject to
great fluctuations; yet there are few or no statistics
available for the guidance of those who are specially
concerned with that branch, or who are considering
the desirability of entering it. The establishment
of Employment Exchanges is a tacit admission of
the need of such statistics, and—though less certainly
—of the duty of the Government to provide them.
Yet even if they were provided it seems beyond dispute
that, in the absence of strong pressure or compulsion
from the State, the choice of individuals would not
always be in accordance with the national needs. The
entry to certain professions—for instance that of medicine—is most properly safeguarded by regulations and
restrictions imposed by bodies to which the State has
delegated certain powers and duties. It may happen
that in one of these professions the number of members
is greatly in excess, or falls far short of the national

requirements; yet neither State nor Professional Council has power to refuse admission to any duly qualified candidate, or to compel certain selected people to undergo the training necessary for qualification. It is quite conceivable, however, that circumstances might arise which would render such action not merely desirable but absolutely essential to the national well-being; indeed it is at least arguable that such circumstances have already arisen. The popular doctrine of the early Victorian era, that the welfare of the community could best be secured by allowing every man to seek his own interests in the way chosen by himself, has been greatly modified or wholly abandoned. So far are we from believing that national efficiency is to be attained by individual liberty that some are in real danger of regarding the two as essentially antagonistic. The nation, as a whole, supported the Legislature in the establishment of compulsory military service; it did so without enthusiasm and only because of the general conviction that such a policy was demanded by the magnitude of the issues at stake. Britons have always been ready, even eager, to give their lives for their country; but, even now, most of them prefer that the obligation to do so should be a moral, rather than a legal one. The doctrine of individual liberty implies the minimum of State interference. Hence there is no country in the world where so much has been left to individual initiative and voluntary effort as in England; and, though of late the number of Government officials has greatly increased, it still remains true that an enormous amount of important work, of a kind which is elsewhere done by salaried servants of the State, is in the hands of voluntary associations or of men who, though appointed or recognised by the State, receive no salary for their services. Nor can it be denied that the work has been, on the whole, well done. A traditional practice of such a kind cannot be (and ought not to be) abandoned at once or without careful consideration; yet the changed conditions of domestic and international politics render some modification necessary.

If the Legislature has protected the purchaser— in spite of the doctrine of "caveat emptor"—by enactments against adulteration of food, and has in addition, created machinery to enforce those enactments, are not we justified in asking that it shall also protect us against incompetence, especially in cases where the effects, though not so obvious, are even more harmful to the community than those which spring from impure food? The prevention of overcrowding in occupations would seem to be the business of the State quite as much as is the prevention of overcrowding in dwelling-houses and factories. The best interests of the nation demand that the entrance to the teaching profession— to take one example out of many—should be safeguarded at least as carefully as the entrance to medicine or law. The supreme importance of the functions exercised by teachers is far from being generally realised, even by teachers themselves; yet upon the effective realisation of that importance the future welfare of the nation largely depends. Doubtless most of us would prefer that the supply of teachers should be maintained by voluntary enlistment, and that their training should be undertaken, like that of medical students, by institutions which owe their origin to private or public beneficence rather than to the State; nevertheless, the obligation to secure adequate numbers of suitable candidates and to provide for their professional training rests ultimately on the State. The obligation has been partially recognised as far as elementary education is concerned, but it is by no means confined to that branch.

It is well to realise at this point that the efficient discharge of the duty thus imposed will of necessity involve a much greater degree of compulsion on both teachers and pupils than has hitherto been employed. The terrible spectacle of the unutilised resources of humanity, which everywhere confronts us in the larger relations of our national life, has been responsible for certain tentatives which have either failed altogether to achieve their object, or have been but partially successful. Much has been heard of the educational ladder—incidentally it may be noted that the educational sieve is equally necessary, though not equally popular—and some attempts have been made to enable a boy or girl of parts to climb from the elementary school to the university without excessive difficulty. To supplement the glaring deficiencies of elementary education a few — ridiculously few — continuation schools have been established. That these and similar measures have failed of success is largely due to the fact that the State has been content to provide facilities, but has refrained from exercising that degree of compulsion which alone could ensure that they would be utilised by those for whose benefit they were created. "Such continuation schools as England possesses," says a German critic, "are without the indispensable condition of compulsion." The reforms recently outlined by the President of the Board of Education show that he, at any rate, admits the criticism to be well grounded. A system which compels a child to attend school until he is fourteen and then leaves him to his own resources can do little to create, and less to satisfy, a thirst for knowledge. During the most critical years of his life—fourteen to eighteen—he is left without guidance, without discipline, without ideals, often without even the desire of remembering or using the little he knows. He is led, as it were, to the threshold of the temple, but the fast-closed door forbids him to enter and behold the glories of the interior. Year by year there is an appalling waste of good human material; and thousands of those whom nature intended to be captains of industry are relegated, in consequence of undeveloped or imperfectly trained capacity, to the ranks, or become hewers of wood and drawers of water. Many drift with other groups of human wastage to the unemployed, thence to the unemployable, and so to the gutter and the grave. The poor we have always with us; but the wastrel—like the pauper—"is a work of art, the creation of wasteful sympathy and legislative inefficiency."

We must be careful, however, in speaking of "the State" to avoid the error of supposing that it is a divinely appointed entity, endowed with power and wisdom from on high. It is, in short, the nation in miniature. Even if the Legislature were composed exclusively of the highest wisdom, the most enlightened patriotism in the country, its enactments must needs fall short of its own standards, and be but little in advance of those of the average of the nation. It must still acknowledge with Solon "These are not the best laws I could make, but they are the best which my nation is fitted to receive." We cannot blame the State without, in fact, condemning ourselves. The absence of any widespread enthusiasm for education, or appreciation of its possibilities; the claims of vested interests; the exigencies of Party Government; and, above all, the murderous tenacity of individual rights have proved well-nigh insuperable obstacles in the path of true educational reform. On the whole we have received as good laws as we have deserved. The changed conditions due to the war, and the changed temper of the nation afford a unique opportunity for wiser counsels, and—to some extent— a guarantee that they shall receive careful and sympathetic consideration.

It may be objected, however, that in taking the teaching profession to exemplify the duty of the State to assume responsibility for both individual and community, we have chosen a case which is exceptional rather than typical; that many, perhaps most, of the other vocations may be safely left to themselves, or, at least left to develop along their own lines with the minimum of State interference. It cannot be denied that there is force in these objections. It should suffice, however, to remark that, if the duty of the State to secure the efficiency of its members in their several callings be admitted, the question of the extent to which, and the manner in which control is exercised is one of detail rather than of principle, and may therefore be settled by the common sense and practical experience of the parties chiefly concerned.

A much more difficult problem is sure to arise, sooner or later, in connection with the utilisation of efficients. Some few years ago the present Prime Minister called attention to the waste of power involved in the training of the rich. They receive, he said, the best that money can buy; their bodies and brains are disciplined; and then "they devote themselves to a life of idleness." It is "a stupid waste of first-class material." Instead of contributing to the work of the world, they "kill their time by tearing along roads at perilous speed, or do nothing at enormous expense." It has needed the bloodiest war in history to reveal the splendid heroism latent in young men of this class. Who can withhold from them gratitude, honour, nay even reverence? But the problem still remains how are the priceless qualities, which have been so freely devoted to the national welfare on the battlefield, to be utilised for the greater works of peace which await us? Are we to recognise the right to be idle as well as the right to work? Is there to be a kind of second Thellusson Act, directed against accumulations of leisure? Or are we to attempt the discovery of some great principle of Conservation of Spiritual Energy, by the application of which these men may make a contribution worthy of themselves to the national life and character? Who can answer?

But though it is freely admitted on all hands that some check upon aggressive individualism is imperatively necessary, and that it is no longer possible to rely entirely upon voluntary organisations however useful, there are not a few of our countrymen who view with grave concern any increase in the power and authority of the State. They point out that such increase tends inevitably towards the despotism of an oligarchy, and that such a despotism, however benevolent in its inception, ruthlessly sacrifices individual interests and liberty to the real or supposed good of the State; that even where constitutional forms remain the spirit which animated them has departed; that officialism and bureaucracy with their attendant evils become supreme, and that the national character steadily deteriorates. They warn us that we may pay too high a price even for organisation and efficiency; and, though it is natural that we should admire certain qualities which we do not possess, we ought not to overlook the fact that those methods which have produced the most perfect national organisation in the history of the world are also responsible for orgies of brutality without parallel among civilised peoples. That such warnings are needful cannot be doubted; but may it not be urged that they indicate dangers incident to a course of action rather than the inevitable consequences thereof? In adapting ourselves to new conditions we must needs take risks. No British Government could stamp out voluntaryism even if it wished to do so; and none has yet manifested any such desire. The nation does not want that kind of national unity of which Germany is so proud, and which seems so admirably adapted to her needs; for the English character and genius rest upon a conception of freedom which renders such a unity foreign and even repulsive to its temper. Whatever be the changes which lie before us, the worship of the State is the one form of idolatry into which the British people are least likely to fall.

II

The recent adaptation of factories and workshops to the production of war material is only typical of what goes on year by year in peace time, though, of course, to a less degree and in less dramatic fashion. Not only are men constantly adapting themselves and their machinery to changed conditions of production, but they are applying the experience and skill gained in the pursuit of one occupation to the problems of another for which it has been exchanged. The comparative ease with which this is done is evidence of the widespread existence of that gift which our enemies call the power of "muddling through," but which has been termed—without wholly sacrificing truth to politeness—the "concurrent adaptability to environment." The British sailor as "handy man" has few equals and no superiors, and he is, in some sort, typical of the nation. The testimony of Thucydides to Themistocles (κράτιστος δὴ οὗτος αὐτοσχεδιάζειν τὰ δέοντα ἐγένετο) might with equal or even greater truth be applied to many Englishmen to-day. As this power αὐτοσχεδιάζειν τὰ δέοντα in the present war saved the Allies from defeat at the outset, so we hope and believe it will carry them on to victory at the last. Yet it becomes a snare if it leads its possessor to neglect preparation or despise organisation, for neither of which can it ever be an entirely satisfactory substitute, albeit a very costly one. At the same time we should recognise that any system of training which seriously impairs this power tends to deprive us of one of the most valuable of our national assets. It follows that, for the majority at least, exclusive or excessive specialisation in training—vocational or otherwise—so far from being an advantage, is a positive drawback; for, as we have seen, a large proportion of our youth manifest no marked bent in any particular direction, and of those who do but a small proportion are capable of that hypertrophy which the highest specialisation demands.

It is important to remember that, though school life is a preparation for practical life, vocational education ought not to begin until a comparatively late stage in a boy's career, if indeed it begins at all while he remains at school. On this it would seem that all professional bodies are agreed; for the entrance examinations, which they have accepted or established are all framed to test a boy's general education and not his knowledge of the special subjects to which he will afterwards devote himself. The evils of premature specialisation are too well known to require even enumeration, and they are increased rather than diminished if that premature specialisation is vocational. The importance of technical training as the means whereby a man is enabled rightly to use the hours of work can hardly be exaggerated; but the value of his work, his worth to his fellows, and his rank in the scale of manhood depend, to at least an equal degree, upon the way in which he uses the hours of leisure. It is one of the greatest of the many functions of a good school to train its members to a wise use of leisure; and though this is not always achieved by direct means the result is none the less valuable. In every calling there must needs be much of what can only be to all save its most enthusiastic devotees—and, at times, even to them—dull routine and drudgery. A man cannot do his best, or be his best, unless he is able to overcome the paralysing influences thus brought to bear upon him by securing mental and spiritual freshness and stimulus; in other words his "inward man must be renewed day by day." There are many agencies which may contribute to such a result; but school memories, school friendships, school "interests" take a foremost place among them. Many boys by the time they leave school have developed an interest or hobby—literary, scientific or practical; and the hobby has an ethical, as well as an economic value. Nor is this all. Excessive devotion to "Bread Studies," whether voluntary or compulsory, tends to make a man's vocation the prison of his soul. Professor Eucken recently told his countrymen that the greater their perfection in work grew, the smaller grew their souls. Any rational interest, therefore, which helps a man to shake off his fetters, helps also to preserve his humanity and to keep him in touch with his fellows. Dr A. C. Benson tells of a distinguished Frenchman who remarked to him, "In France a boy goes to school or college, and perhaps does his best. But he does not get the sort of passion for the honour and prosperity of his school or college which you English seem to feel." It is this wondrous faculty of inspiring unselfish devotion which makes our schools the spiritual power-houses of the nation. This love for an abstraction, which even the dullest boys feel, is the beginning of much that makes English life sweet and pure. It is the same spirit which, in later years, moves men to do such splendid voluntary work for their church, their town, their country, and even in some cases leads them "to take the whole world for their parish."

However much we may strive to reach the beautiful Montessori ideal, the fact remains that there must be some lessons, some duties, which the pupil heartily dislikes and would gladly avoid if he could; but they must be done promptly and satisfactorily, and, if not cheerfully, at least without audible murmuring. Eventually he may, and often does, come to like them; at any rate he realises that they are not set before him in order to irritate or punish him, but as part of his school training. It will be agreed that the acquirement of a habit of doing distasteful things, even under compulsion, because they are part of one's duty is no bad preparation for a life in which most days bring their quota of unpleasant duties which cannot be avoided, delegated, or postponed.

At the present time, however, there is a real danger—in some quarters at least—of unduly emphasising the specifically vocational, or "practical" side of education. The man of affairs knows little or nothing of young minds and their limitations, of the conditions under which teaching is done, or of the educational values of the various studies in a school curriculum. He is prone to choose subjects chiefly or solely because of their immediate practical utility. Thus in his view the chief reason for learning a modern language is that business communications will thereby be facilitated. One could wish that he would be content to indicate the end which he has in view, and which he sees clearly, and leave the means of obtaining it to the judgment and experience of the teacher; for in education, as in other spheres of action, the obvious way is rarely the right way, and very often the way of disaster. Yet it is a distinct gain to have the practical man brought into the administration of educational affairs; for teachers are, as a rule, too little in contact with the world of commerce to know much of the needs and ideas of business men. The Board of Education has already established a Consultative Committee of Educationists. Why should not a similar standing Committee, consisting of representatives of the Chambers of Commerce of the country be also appointed? Such a Committee could render, as could no other body, invaluable service to the cause of education.

From a recent article by Professor Leacock we

learn that some twenty years ago there was a considerable change in the Canadian schools and universities. "The railroad magnate, the corporation manager, the promoter, the multiform director, and all the rest of the group known as captains of industry, began to besiege the universities clamouring for practical training for their sons." Mr Leacock tells of a "great and famous Canadian public school," which he attended, at which practical banking was taught so resolutely that they had wire gratings and little wickets, books labelled with the utmost correctness, and all manner of real-looking things. It all came to an end, and now it appears that in Canada they are beginning to find that the great thing is to give a schoolboy a mind that will do anything; when the time comes "you will train your banker in a bank." It may be that everybody has not recognised this, and that the railroad magnates and the rest of them are not yet fully convinced; but Mr Leacock declares that the most successful schools of commerce will not now attempt to teach the mechanism of business, because "the solid, orthodox studies of the university programme, taken in suitable, selective groups, offer the most practical training in regard to intellectual equipment, that the world has yet devised."

To the same purport is the evidence given by Mr H. A. Roberts, Secretary of the Cambridge Appointments Board (see *Minutes of Evidence taken before the Royal Commission on the Civil Service,* *22nd November* 1912–13*th December* 1912, pp. 66–73). The whole of this testimony deserves careful study.

For some few years past the heads of the great business firms, in this country and abroad, have been applying in ever increasing numbers to Cambridge (and to Oxford also, though in this case statistics do not appear to be available) for men to take charge of departments and agencies; to become, in fact, "captains of industry." In the year before the war (1913–14) about 135 men were transferred from Cambridge University to commercial posts through the agency of the Board[1]. One might naturally suppose that the majority of these were science men; on the contrary, owing no doubt to the greater number of other posts open to them, they were fewer than might have been expected. Graduates from every Tripos are found in the 135 in numbers roughly proportional to the numbers in the various Tripos lists. Shortly before the war an advertisement of an important managership of some works—in South America, if I remember rightly—ended with the intimation that, other things being equal, preference would be given to a man who had taken a good degree in Classical Honours.

That most of such men are successful in their occupations might be deemed to be proved by the steady increase in the number of applications made for their services. There is, however, more definite evidence available. A member of one of the largest business firms in the country testified to the same Royal Commission that of the 46 Cambridge men who

[1] In this connection it may be noted that 43 per cent. of the members of Trinity College—where the normal number of undergraduates in residence is over 600—on leaving the university devote themselves to business.

had been taken into his employment during the previous seven years 43 had done excellently well, two had left before their probationary period was ended to take up other work; and one only had proved unsatisfactory. This evidence could easily be supplemented did space permit. It is clear, then, that in many callings what is wanted—to begin with, at any rate—is not so much technical knowledge as trained intelligence.

Another reason for thus choosing university men is not difficult to discover. When Mr W. L. Hichens (Chairman of Cammell, Laird and Co.) addressed the Incorporated Association of Headmasters in January last he declared that in choosing university graduates for business he looked out for the man who might have got a First in Greats or history, if he had worked —a man who had other interests as well, who was President of the Common Room, who had been pleasant in the Common Room, or on the river, or rowed in his college "Eight," or had done something else which showed that he could get on with his fellow-men. In business getting on means getting on with men.

The experience of Mr Hichens is so valuable that I cannot do better than quote further. "A big industrial organisation such as my firm, has, or should have three main sub-divisions—the manufacturing branch, the commercial branch, and the research or laboratory branch....I will not deal with the rank and file, but with the better educated apprentices, who expect to rise to positions of responsibility. On the workshop side, we prefer that the lads should come to us between sixteen and seventeen, and, if possible (after serving an apprenticeship in the shops and drawing office), that they should then go to a university and take an engineering course.

"On the commercial side also we prefer to get the boys between sixteen and seventeen. We have recently, however, reserved a limited number of vacancies for university men. The research department also is, in the main, recruited from university men. But there is this difference, that, whereas the research men should have received a scientific training at the university we require no specialised education in the case of university men joining the commercial side. Specialised education at school is of no practical value. There is ample time after a boy has started business to acquire all the technical knowledge that his brain is capable of assimilating. What we want when we take a boy is to assure ourselves that he has ability and moral strength of character, and I submit that the true function of education is to teach him how to learn and how to live—not how to make a living. We are interested naturally to know that a boy has an aptitude for languages or mathematics, but it is immaterial to us whether he has acquired his aptitude, say for learning languages, through learning Latin and Greek or French and German. The educational value is paramount, the vocational negligible. If, therefore, modern languages are taught because they will be useful in later life, while Latin and Greek are omitted because they have no practical use, although their educational value may be greater, you will be bartering away the boy's rightful heritage of knowledge for a mess of pottage."

There are doubtless many different opinions as to the best way of training boys to become engineers, and in giving the results of his experience Mr Hichens does not claim that he is voicing the unanimous and well-considered judgments of the whole profession. His statement that "specialised education at school is of no practical value to us" would certainly be challenged by those schools which possess a strong, well-organised engineering side for their elder boys. But there would be substantial unanimity—begotten of long and often bitter experience—in favour of his plea that a sound general education up to the age of sixteen or seventeen at any rate, is an indispensable condition of satisfactory vocational training. "I venture to think," says Mr Hichens, "that the tendency of modern education is often in the wrong direction—that too little attention is given to the foundations which lie buried out of sight, below the ground, and too much to a showy superstructure. We pay too much heed to the parents who want an immediate return in kind on their money, and forget that education consists in tilling the ground and sowing the seed—forget, too, that the seed must grow of itself."

It would appear from what has already been said that though the necessity for vocational training exists in most, if not in all cases, the time in a boy's life at which such training ought to begin is far from being the same for all callings. Even where there is general agreement as to the normal age, exceptional circumstances or exceptional ability may justify the postponement of vocational instruction to a much later period than would usually be desirable. Thus the fact that two of the most distinguished members of the medical profession graduated as Senior Wrangler and Senior Classic respectively, will not justify the average medical student in waiting until he is twenty-three before commencing his professional training. If it be true that in some quarters "specialised education" has been demanded for young boys, it is equally true that many youths pass through school and enter the university without any clear idea of whither they are tending. This uncertainty may be due to a belief that "something is sure to turn up," to the magnitude of their allowances and the ease of their circumstances, occasionally, perhaps, to excessive timidity or underestimation of their powers; but, from whatever cause it springs, such an attitude of mind is deplorable in itself, and fraught with grave moral dangers. It ought to be possible in the case of a boy of sixteen or seventeen to say with some approach to certainty, for what employments he is quite unsuitable, and to indicate the general direction, at least, in which he should seek his life-work. The *onus* of choice is too often laid upon the boy himself; and the form in which the question is put—What would you *like* to be?—makes him the judge not only of his own desires and abilities, but also of the conditions of callings with which he can, at best, be but imperfectly acquainted. There is here fine scope for the co-operation of parents and teachers not only with each other but with the various professional and business organisations. It is generally supposed to be the duty of a head master to observe and study the boys committed to his care. It is equally important that he should extend that study and observation to their parents—as an act of justice to the boys, if for no other reason. But there are other reasons. There is knowledge to be gotten from every parent—or at least from every father—about his profession or business—knowledge which, as a rule, he is quite willing to impart. If, in addition, a head master avails himself of the opportunities of getting into touch with men of affairs, leaders of commerce, professional men of all kinds, his advice to parents as to suitable careers for their sons becomes enormously more valuable. At the very least he may save them from some of the more flagrant forms of error; for instance, he may convince them that there are other and more valuable indications of fitness for engineering than the ability to take a bicycle to pieces, and a desire "to see the wheels go round"; and that a boy who is "good at sums" will not, of necessity, make a good accountant. In short, he may prevent them from mistaking a hobby for a vocation.

III

It ought to be clearly stated that in writing of schools I have had in mind those which are usually known as public schools; for in the general preparation for practical life the public school boy enjoys many advantages which do not fall to the lot of his less-favoured brother in the elementary school. Not only does his education continue for some years longer, but it is conducted along broader lines, and gives him a greater variety of knowledge and a wider outlook. He comes, too, as a rule, from those classes of the community in which there are long standing traditions of discipline, culture, and what may be called the spirit of *noblesse oblige*. These traditions do not, of themselves, keep him from folly, idleness, or even vice; but they do help him to endure hardship, to submit to authority, to cultivate the corporate spirit, to maintain certain standards of schoolboy honour, and, as he himself would say, "to play the game." Though in the class-room it may be that appeals are largely made to individualism and selfishness, yet on the playing fields he learns something of the value of co-operation and the virtue of unselfishness. From the very first he begins to develop a sense of civic and collective responsibility, and, in his later years at school, he finds that as a prefect or monitor he has a direct share in the government of the community of which he is a member, and a direct responsibility for its welfare. Nor does this sense of corporate life die out when he leaves, for then the Old Boys' Association claims him, and adds a new interest to the past, while maintaining the old inspiration for the future.

With the elementary school boy it is not so. To him, as to his parents, the primal curse is painfully real: work is the sole and not always effectual means of warding off starvation. He realises that as soon as the law permits he is to be "turned into money" and must needs become a wage-earner. As a contributor to the family exchequer he claims a voice in his own government, and resists all the attempts of parents, masters, or the State itself to encroach upon his liberty. He begins work with both mind and body immature and ill-trained. There has been little to teach him *esprit de corps*; he has never felt the sobering influence of responsibility; the only discipline he has experienced is that of the class-room, for the O.T.C. and organised games are to him unknown; and when he leaves there is very rarely any Association of Old Boys to keep him in touch with his fellows or the school. Here and there voluntary organisations such as the Boy Scouts have done something—though little—to improve his lot; but, in the main, the evils are untouched. To find the remedy for them is not the least of the many great problems of the future.

The improvement of any one branch of industry ultimately means the improvement of those engaged therein. Scientific agriculture, for example, is hardly possible until we have scientific agriculturists. In like manner real success in practical life depends on the temper and character of the practitioner even more than upon his technical equipment. There are, however, three great obstacles to the progress of the nation as a whole, obstacles which can only be removed very gradually, and by the continuous action of many moral forces. We are far too little concerned with intellectual interests. "No nation, I imagine," says Mr Temple, "has ever gone so far as England in its

214 Sir J. D. McClure: Preparation for Practical Life

neglect of and contempt for the intellect. If goodness
of character means the capacity to serve our nation
as useful citizens, it is unobtainable by any one who
is content to let his mind slumber." Then again we
suffer from the low ideal which leads us to worship
success. From his earliest years a boy learns from his
surroundings, if not by actual precept, to strive not
so much to be something as somebody. The love of
power rather than fame may be the "last infirmity of
noble minds," but it is probably the first infirmity of
many ignoble ones. Herein lies the justification of
the criticism of a friendly alien. "You pride your-
selves on your incorruptibility, and quite rightly; for
in England there is probably less actual bribery by
means of money than in any other country. *But
you can all be bribed by power.*" Lastly (to quote
Mr Hichens yet once more), "Strong pressure is being
brought to bear to commercialise our education, to
make it a paying proposition, to make it subservient
to the God of Wealth and thus convert us into a money-
making mob. Ruskin has said that 'no nation can
last that has made a mob of itself.' Above all a nation
cannot last as a money-making mob. It cannot with
impunity—it cannot with existence—go on despising
literature, despising science, despising art, despising
nature, despising compassion, and concentrating its
soul on pence."

XI

TEACHING AS A PROFESSION

By FRANK ROSCOE
Secretary of the Teachers Registration Council

The title of this chapter is prophetic rather than descriptive for although teachers often claim for their work a professional status and find their claim recognised by the common use of the phrase "teaching profession" yet it must be admitted that teachers do not form a true professional body. They include in their ranks instructors of all types, from the university professor to the private teacher or "professor" of music. Their terms of engagement and rate of remuneration exhibit every possible variety. Their fitness to undertake the work of teaching is not tested specifically, save in the case of certain classes of teachers in public elementary schools, nor is there any general agreement as to the proper nature and scope of such a test, could one be devised. Usually, it is true, the prospective employer demands evidence that the intending teacher has some knowledge of the subject he is to teach. He may seek to satisfy himself that the applicant has other desirable qualities, personal and physical, which will fit him to take an active and useful part in school work. These inquiries, however, will have little or no reference to his skill in teaching, apart from what is called discipline or form management.

The characteristics of a true profession are not easily defined, but it may be assumed that they include the existence of a body of scientific principles as the foundation of the work and the exercise of some measure of control by the profession itself in regard to the qualifications of those who seek to enter its ranks. Taken together, these two characteristics may be said to mark off a true profession from a business or trade. The skilled craftsman or artisan may belong to a union which seeks to control the entrance to its ranks, but the difference between the member of the Amalgamated Society of Engineers and the member of the Institution of Mechanical Engineers is that the former belongs to a body chiefly concerned with the application of certain methods while the latter belongs to one which is concerned with those methods, not only in their application but also in their origin and development.   It is recognised that there is a body of scientific knowledge underlying the practice of engineering, and the various professional institutions of engineers seek to extend this knowledge, while claiming also the right to ascertain the qualifications of those who desire to become members of their profession.   The same is true in different ways with regard to the professions of law and medicine.   It is to be noted also that within these professions the admitted member is on a footing of equality with all his colleagues save only so far as his professional skill and eminence entitle him to special consideration.

It will be seen at once that there are great difficulties to be overcome before teaching can be truly described as a profession. The diversity of the work is so great that it may be held that teaching is not one calling but a blend of many. It is difficult to find any common link between the university professor, the head master of a great public school, an instructor in physical training, and a kindergarten teacher. It is not easy to bring together the head master of a preparatory school, working in complete independence, and the head master of a public elementary school, dealing with pupils of about the same age as those in the preparatory school, but controlled and directed by an elected public authority under the general supervision of the Board of Education. Yet despite these apparent divergences of aim all teachers may be regarded as pursuing the same end. They are engaged in bringing to bear upon their pupils certain formal and purposeful influences with the object of enabling them to play their part in the business of life. Such formal influences are seconded by countless informal ones. School and university alone do not make the complete man and it is an important part of the teacher's task to second his direct and purposeful teaching by the influence of his own personality and conduct, and by securing that the form or school is in harmony with the general aim of his work.

Skill in imparting instruction is by no means the whole of the equipment required by a teacher. It is indeed possible to give "a good lesson" or a series of "good lessons" and yet to fail in the real work of teaching. In some branches far too much stress has been laid on the more purely technical and mechanical attributes of good teaching as distinct from the finer and more permanent qualities such as intellectual stimulus, the awakening of a spirit of inquiry, and the development of a true corporate sense. By way of excuse it may be said that teaching has tended to become a form of drill chiefly in those schools where the classes have been too large to permit of anything better than rigid discipline and a constant attention to the learning of facts. Teachers in such circumstances are gravely handicapped in all the more enduring and important parts of their work. Very large schools and classes of an unwieldy size tend to turn the teacher into a mere drill sergeant.

While full provision should always be made for the exercise of the teacher's individuality there must be sought some unifying principle in all forms of teaching work. Unless it is agreed that the imparting of instruction demands special skill as distinct from knowledge of the subject-matter we shall be driven to accept the view that the teacher, as such, deserves no more consideration than any casual worker. No claim to rank as a profession can be maintained on behalf of teachers if it is held that their work may be undertaken with no more preparation than is involved in the study of the subject or subjects they purpose to teach. A true profession implies a ''mystery'' or at least an art or craft and some knowledge of this would seem to be essential for teachers if they are to have professional status.

The difficulty in this connection is that the principles of teaching have not yet been worked out satisfactorily. Our knowledge of the operations of the mind develops very slowly and those who carry out investigations in this field of research are few in number. Their conclusions are not necessarily related to teaching practice but cover a wider field. The study of applied psychology with special reference to the work of the teacher needs to be encouraged since it will serve to enlarge that body of scientific principle which should form the basis of teaching work. It is by no means necessary, or even desirable, that teachers should be expected to spend their time in psychological research. Their business is to teach and this requires that they should devote themselves to applying in practice the truths ascertained and verified by the psychologists. For this purpose it will be necessary that they should know something of the method by which these truths are sought and proved. It is also an advantage for teachers to learn something of the history of education, not as a series of biographies of so-called Great Educators but rather with the object of learning what has been suggested and attempted in former times. Such a knowledge furnishes the teacher with the necessary power to deal with new proposals and with the many "systems" and "methods" which are continually arising. Instead of becoming an eager advocate of every novelty or adopting an attitude of indiscriminate scepticism he will be in some measure able to estimate the true merit of new proposals, and his knowledge of mental operations will serve as an aid in judging whether they have any germ of sound principle. The alternative plan of leaving the teacher to learn his craft solely by practice often has the result of confining him too closely to narrow and stereotyped methods, based either on the imperfect recollection of his own schooldays, or on the method of some other teacher. Imitation is cramping and serves to destroy the qualities of initiative and adaptability which are indispensable to success in teaching.

It will be noted that no extravagant demand is put forward on behalf of what is called training in teaching. The methods of training hitherto practised have been based too frequently on the assumption that it is possible to fashion a teacher from the outside, as it were, by causing him to attend lectures on psychology and teaching method and to hear a course of demonstration lessons. This plan may fail completely since it is possible to write excellent examination answers on the subjects named and even to give a prepared lesson reasonably well without being fitted to undertake the charge of a form. It should be recognised that the practice of teaching can be acquired only in the class-room under conditions which are normal and therefore entirely different from those existing in the practising school of a training college. When this truth is fully apprehended we may expect to find that the young teacher is required to spend his first year in a school where the head master and one or more members of the regular staff are qualified to guide his early efforts and to establish the necessary link between his knowledge of theory and his requirements in practice.

The Departments of Education in the universities should be encouraged to develop systematic research into the principles of teaching and should be in close touch with the schools in which teachers are receiving their practical training.

The plan suggested will be free from the reproach often levelled against the existing method of training teachers, namely, that it is too theoretical and produces people who can talk glibly about education without being able to manage a class. It will also recognise the truth that the young teacher has much to learn in regard to the art or craft of teaching and that there are certain general principles which he must know and follow if he is to be successful in his chosen work. The application of these principles to his own circumstances is a matter of practice, for in teaching, as in any other art, the element of personality far outweighs in its importance any matter of formal technique or special method. The ascertained and accepted principles underlying all teaching should be known and thereafter the teacher should develop his own method, reflecting in his practice the bent of his mind.

The recognition of a principle does not of necessity involve uniformity in practice. Freedom in execution is possible only within the limits of an art. The problem is to define these limits in such a liberal manner as will allow for variety and individual expression. The saying that teachers are born, not made, is one which may be made of those who practise any art, but the poet or painter can exercise his innate gifts only within certain limits and with regard to certain rules. It is no less fatal to his art for him to abandon all rules than it is for him to accept every rule slavishly and apply it to himself without intelligence.

The acceptance of the principle that there is an art or at least a craft of teaching is a condition precedent to any attempt to make teaching a profession in reality as well as in name.

The further requirement is that those who are engaged in teaching should have some power of controlling the conditions under which they work and more especially of testing the qualifications of those who desire to join their ranks. This demands a recognition of the essential unity of all teaching work and a consequent effort to bring all teachers together as members of one body, possessing a certain unity or solidarity in spite of its apparent diversities. To form such a body is a task of great difficulty since the various types of teachers have in the past tended to separate themselves into groups, each having its own association and machinery for the protection of its own interests. Apart from the teaching staffs of the various universities, there are in England and Wales over fifty associations of teachers, ranging from the National Union of Teachers with over ninety thousand subscribing members to bodies numbering only a few score adherents. These associations reflect the great diversity of teaching work already described, but all alike are seeking to promote freedom for the teacher in his work and to advance professional objects. Such aspirations have been in the minds of teachers for many years and from time to time attempts have been made to realise them by establishing a professional Council with its necessary adjunct of a Register of qualified persons. Seventy years ago the College of Preceptors, with its grades of Associate, Licentiate and Fellow, suggesting a comparison with the College of Physicians, was established with the object of "raising the standard of the profession by providing a guarantee of fitness and respectability." The College Register was to contain the names of all those who were qualified to conduct schools, and admission to the Register was controlled by the College itself in order to provide a means of excluding all who were likely to bring discredit upon the calling of a teacher by reason of their inefficiency or misconduct. The scheme thus launched was, however, not comprehensive, since it concerned chiefly the teachers who conducted private schools and did not contemplate the inclusion of those who were engaged in universities, public schools, or the elementary schools working under the then recently established scheme of State grants. Teachers in schools of this last description were apparently intended by the government of the day to be regarded as civil servants, appointed and paid by the State. Subsequent legislation modified this arrangement, but teachers in schools receiving government grants are still subject to a measure of control, and those in public elementary schools are licensed by the State before being allowed to teach. It will be seen that the effort to organise a teaching profession was hampered from the start by the fact that teachers were not entirely free to set up their own conditions, since the State had already taken charge of one branch, while further difficulties arose from the varied character of different forms of teaching work and from the circumstance that some of these forms were traditionally associated with membership of another profession, that of a clergyman.

Hence it was that despite several attempts to institute a Register of Teachers and to organise a profession the difficulties seemed to be insurmountable. Between the years 1869 and 1899 several bills were introduced in Parliament with the object of setting up a Register of Teachers but all met with opposition and were abandoned. The Board of Education Act of 1899 gave powers for constituting by Order in Council a Consultative Committee to advise the Board on any matter referred to the Committee and also to frame, with the approval of the Board, regulations for a Register of Teachers. It was not until 1902 that an Order in Council established a Registration Council and laid down regulations for the institution of a Register. The Council thus established consisted of twelve members, six of whom were nominated by the President of the Board of Education while one was elected by each of the following bodies: the Headmasters' Conference, the Headmasters' Association, the Head Mistresses' Association, the College of Preceptors, the Teachers' Guild, and the National Union of Teachers. The members of the Council were to hold office for three years, and afterwards, on 1 April,

1905, the constitution of the Council was to be revised. The duty assigned to the Council was that of establishing and keeping a Register of Teachers in accordance with the regulations framed by the Consultative Committee and approved by the Board of Education. Subject to the approval of the Board the Council was empowered to appoint officers and to pay them. The income was to be provided by fees for registration and the accounts were to be audited and published annually by the Board to whom the Council was also required to submit a report of its proceedings once a year.

Under this scheme a Register was set up, with two columns, A and B. In the former were placed the names of all teachers who had obtained the government certificate as teachers in public elementary schools. This involved no application or payment by such teachers, who were thus registered automatically. Column B was reserved for teachers in secondary schools, public and private. Registration in these cases was voluntary and demanded the payment of a registration fee of one guinea in addition to evidence of acceptable qualification in regard to academic standing and professional training. Although teachers of experience were admitted on easier terms the regulations were intended to ensure that, after a given date, everybody who was accepted for registration should have passed satisfactorily through a course of training in teaching. As designed in the first instance Column B furnished no place for teachers of special subjects and it became necessary to institute supplemental Registers in regard to music and other branches which had come to form part of the ordinary curriculum of a secondary school.

The scheme thus provided a Register divided into groups according to the nature of the accepted applicant's work. Such an arrangement presented many difficulties since it ignored all university teachers and assigned the others to different categories depending in some instances on the type of school in which they chanced to be working and in others on the subject which they happened to be teaching.

A professional Register constructed on these lines had the seeming advantage of supplying information as to the type of work for which the individual teacher was best fitted. On the other hand it was held that the division of teachers into categories was unsound in principle and the teachers in public elementary schools were not slow to resent the suggestion that they belonged to an inferior rank and were properly to be excused the payment of a fee. They pointed out that many of their number held academic qualifications which were higher than those required to secure admission to Column B wherein some eleven thousand teachers had been registered, of whom not more than one half were graduates. The views thus expressed were shared by many other teachers and it speedily became manifest that the proposed Register could not succeed. In the Annual Report of 1905 the Council stated that under existing conditions it was not practicable to frame and publish an alphabetical Register of Teachers such as appeared to be contemplated in the Act of 1899. In June, 1906, the

Board of Education published a memorandum stating the reasons which had led it to take the opportunity afforded by impending legislation to abolish the Register, and in the Education Bill of 1906 a clause was inserted which removed from the Consultative Committee the obligation to frame a Register of Teachers.

This clause was strongly opposed by many associations of teachers. It was urged by these bodies that although one scheme had failed yet a Register was still possible and desirable. It was held by many that the task assigned to the Registration Council had been an impossible one since the conditions of supervision and control imposed under the Act of 1899 left the Council very little freedom and wholly precluded the establishment of a self-governing profession. The general opinion seemed to be that any future Register must be in one column avoiding any attempt to divide those registered into different classes and that any future Council must be as independent and widely representative as possible. This opinion found expression and official sanction in a memorandum issued by the Board of Education in 1911 after several conferences had been held for the purpose of promoting a new registration scheme. The memorandum stated that: "It should not be so much the kinds of teachers likely to be most rapidly or easily admitted to the Register that should specially determine the composition of the Council but rather the larger and more general conception of the unification of the Teaching Profession." This new and wider idea served to govern the formation of the Teachers Registration

Council which was established by an Order in Council
of February, 1912. The body constituted by this
Order consists wholly of teachers and includes eleven
representatives of each of the following classes: the
Teaching Staffs of Universities, the Associations of
Teachers in Public Elementary Schools, the Associations of Teachers in Secondary Schools, and the Associations of Teachers of Specialist Subjects. The Council
thus numbers forty-four and it is ordered that the
chairman shall be elected by the Council from outside
its own body. At least one woman must be elected
by each appointing body which sends more than one
representative to the Council provided that the body
includes women among its members. It will be seen
that the constitution aimed at forming a Council
wholly independent and thoroughly representative.
This quality was further ensured by the establishment
of ten committees, representing various forms of
specialist teaching and providing that any conditions
of registration framed by the Council should be submitted to these committees before publication.

The first Council under this scheme was formed in
1912 and held office for three years as prescribed by
the Order in Council. The chairman was the Right
Honourable A. H. Dyke Acland and the members included the Vice-Chancellors of several universities and
representatives of forty-two associations of teachers.
The first duty of the Council was to devise conditions
of registration and these were framed during 1913,
being published at the end of that year. They provide
in the first place that up to the end of 1920 any teacher

may be admitted to registration who produces evidence of having taught under circumstances approved by the Council for a minimum period of five years. Regard for existing interests led to the setting up of a period of grace before the full conditions of registration came into force. After 1920, however, these become more stringent and require that before being admitted to registration the teacher shall produce evidence of knowledge and experience, while all save university teachers are also required to have undertaken a course of training in teaching. Under both the temporary and later arrangement the minimum age for registration is twenty-five and the fee is a single payment of one guinea. There is no annual subscription.

The second Council was elected in 1915 and appointed as its chairman Dr Michael E. Sadler, Vice-Chancellor of the University of Leeds. Up to the middle of July, 1916, the number of teachers admitted to the Register was 17,628 and the names of these were included in the *Official List of Registered Teachers* issued by the Council at the beginning of 1917. The Register itself is too voluminous for publication since it comprises all the particulars which an accepted applicant has submitted. All registered teachers receive a copy of their own register entry together with a certificate of registration. It will be seen that the task of receiving and considering applications for registration forms an important part of the Council's work. But it is by no means its chief function. As is shown in the Board of Education memorandum already quoted the Council is intended to promote the unification of the teaching profession. The Register is nothing more than the symbol of this unity and the Council is charged with the important task of expressing the views of teachers as a body on all matters concerning their work. This is shown in the speech made by the Minister of Education at the first meeting of the Council. After welcoming the members he added:

"The object of the Council would be not only the formation of a Register of Teachers. There were many other spheres and fields of usefulness for a Council representative of the Teaching Profession. He hoped that they would be able to speak with one voice as representing the Teaching Profession, and that the Board would be able to consult with them. So long as he was head of the Board they would always be most anxious to co-operate with the Council and would attach due weight to their views. He hoped that they on their side would realise some of the Board's difficulties and that the atmosphere of friendly relationship which he trusted had already been established would continue."

The functions of the Council are thus seen to extend beyond the mere compilation of a Register of Teachers and to include constant co-operation with those engaged in educational administration. In view of the desire which is now generally expressed for a closer union between the directive and executive elements in all branches of industry it is safe to assume that the Teachers' Council will grow steadily in importance, especially if it is seen to have the support of all teachers.

Meanwhile it furnishes the framework of a possible

teaching profession and gives promise of securing for the teacher a definite status by establishing a standard of attainment and qualification. More than this will be required, however, if the work of teaching is to be placed on its proper level in public esteem. Those who undertake the work must be led to look for something more than material gain. The teacher needs a sense of vocation no less than the clergyman or doctor. It has been said that "teaching is the noblest of professions but the sorriest of trades" and the absence of any real enthusiasm for the work inevitably produces an attitude of mind which is alien to the spirit of a real teacher. The material reward of the teacher has accurately reflected the want of public esteem attaching to his work. For the most part a meagre pittance has been all that he could anticipate and this has led to a steady decline in the number of recruits. A profession should furnish a reasonable prospect of a career and a fair chance of gaining distinction. Such opportunities have been far too few in teaching to attract able and ambitious young men in adequate number. The remedy is to open every branch of educational work and administration to those who have proved themselves to be efficient teachers. The national welfare demands that those who are to be charged with the task of training future citizens should be drawn from the most able of our young people, to whom teaching should offer a career not less attractive than other callings. In particular the teacher should be regarded as a member of a profession and trusted to carry out his duties in a responsible manner. Excessive supervision and inspection will tend to discourage and eventually destroy that quality of initiative which is indispensable in all teaching. Freed from the monetary cares which now oppress him, definitely established as a member of a profession having some voice in its own concerns, encouraged to exercise his art under conditions of the greatest possible freedom, and provided with reasonable opportunity for advancement, the teacher will be able to take up his work in a new spirit. We may then demand from new-comers a sense of vocation and expect with some justification that teachers will be able to avoid the professional groove which is hardly to be escaped and which is quite inevitable if the conditions of one's work preclude opportunity for maintaining freshness of mind and a variety of personal interest. Such limitations as accompany inadequate salaries, lack of prospects and absence of professional status convert teaching into "a dull mechanic art" and deprive it of its chief elements of enjoyment, namely the free exercise of personality and the recurring satisfaction of seeing minds develop under instruction, so that we are conscious of our part in helping the future citizens to make the most of their lives. It is this power of impressing one's own personality on the pliable mind of youth which brings at once the greatest responsibility and the highest reward to the teacher and attaches to his task a true professional character since it may not be undertaken fittingly by any who cherish low aims or despise their work.